Praise for
The Disappearance of God

"From grade inflation to global calamities, Albert Mohler is a steady guide. From the psychological coddling of the American ego to the hollowing of the American conscience, Mohler is unremittingly clearheaded. From Nineveh to New Orleans, Mohler holds the mirror at a blazing forty-five-degree angle between heaven and earth. The burning light of divine wisdom illumines a hundred shadows of our human folly. And at the center of the blaze is the mighty cross of Jesus Christ defining the final meaning of everything. I thank God for Albert Mohler."

> —JOHN PIPER, pastor for preaching and vision, Bethlehem Baptist Church, Minneapolis, MN

"Al Mohler is a unique gift to the church. His writing combines penetrating theological discernment and insightful cultural analysis with a passion to faithfully proclaim the gospel of Jesus Christ. I'm delighted that Al's wisdom is now available in this book."

> —C. J. MAHANEY, Sovereign Grace Ministries

"In *The Disappearance of God,* Dr. Mohler has provided a striking, biblically based treatment of a coterie of compelling issues which threaten the religious public at every turn. With his usual incisive and scintillating analysis, he sorts out healthy from unhealthy influences and charts a path for future church development. If you are serious about navigating our contemporary world, this is a necessary read."

—PAIGE PATTERSON, president, Southwestern
Baptist Theological Seminary, Fort Worth, TX

"Here is a picture on the life of the church where it is being troubled, seduced, and attacked by today's dominant cultural forces. Its analysis is clear and to the point, and its answers are biblically framed, thoughtful, and helpful. I wish there were more books like this!"

—DAVID F. WELLS, distinguished research professor, Gordon-Conwell Theological Seminary

"There is a paucity of prophetic Christian voices today speaking about the dangerous trends in our churches and culture. Albert Mohler is one of those leading voices who provides clarity and conviction in a culture of ambiguity, aimlessness, and ambivalence. I am thankful for his book *The Disappearance of God* and the clear direction it provides in the murky culture in which we live. Above all, I am thankful for Dr. Mohler and his heart for Christ's church."

—THOM S. RAINER, president and CEO, LifeWay Christian
Resources, and author of *Essential Church* and *Simple Life*

"A remarkably insightful and disturbing analysis of the erosion of belief in God in many strategic centers of influence in today's culture."

—WAYNE GRUDEM, Ph.D. Research Professor of Theology
and Biblical Studies, Phoenix Seminary, Phoenix, AZ

THE DISAPPEARANCE

OF GOD

DANGEROUS BELIEFS
IN THE NEW SPIRITUAL OPENNESS

R. ALBERT MOHLER JR.

MULTNOMAH
BOOKS

THE DISAPPEARANCE OF GOD
PUBLISHED BY MULTNOMAH BOOKS
12265 Oracle Boulevard, Suite 200
Colorado Springs, Colorado 80921

Scripture quotations unless otherwise indicated are taken from the New American Standard Bible®. © Copyright The Lockman Foundation 1960, 1962, 1963, 1968, 1971, 1972, 1973, 1975, 1977, 1995. Used by permission. (www.Lockman.org). Scripture quotations marked (ESV) are taken from The Holy Bible, English Standard Version, copyright © 2001 by Crossway Bibles, a division of Good News Publishers. Used by permission. All rights reserved.

ISBN 978-1-60142-081-7

ISBN 978-1-60142-234-7 (electronic)

Copyright © 2009 by R. Albert Mohler

Published in association with the literary agency of Wolgemuth & Associates Inc.

Published in the United States by WaterBrook Multnomah, an imprint of the Crown Publishing Group, a division of Random House Inc., New York.

MULTNOMAH and its mountain colophon are registered trademarks of Random House Inc.

Library of Congress Cataloging-in-Publication Data
Mohler, R. Albert, 1959–
    The disappearance of God : dangerous beliefs in the new spiritual openness / R. Albert Mohler, Jr.—1st ed.
        p. cm.
    ISBN 978-1-60142-081-7—ISBN 978-1-60142-234-7 (electronic)
1. Evangelicalism. 2. Liberalism (Religion) I. Title.
    BR1640.M65 2009
    270.8'3—dc22

                                                    2008050184

Printed in the United States of America
2010

10 9 8 7 6 5 4 3 2

SPECIAL SALES
Most WaterBrook Multnomah books are available at special quantity discounts when purchased in bulk by corporations, organizations, and special-interest groups. Custom imprinting or excerpting can also be done to fit special needs. For information, please e-mail SpecialMarkets@WaterBrookMultnomah.com or call 1-800-603-7051.

CONTENTS

To Christopher Albert Mohler
Son by the flesh, brother in the Spirit, delight of his parents,
friend of my heart

ACKNOWLEDGMENTS

With very rare exceptions, books represent a conversation. This is certainly true in the case of this book. I am deeply indebted to the many persons with whom I have discussed the issues and doctrines and controversies considered in this volume. In particular, I owe a debt to the faculty of The Southern Baptist Theological Seminary and Boyce College. These dedicated colleagues represent such a faithful corps of Christian thinkers and teachers.

I also want to thank the many students I have taught in the classroom. In the course of instruction, no one learns more than the teacher. Likewise, I thank my student interns, whose intelligence and interest are great gifts.

I gladly acknowledge the invaluable assistance rendered by Scott Lamb, director of research in my office. His help in getting this project ready for publication is greatly appreciated. I also want to thank Jason Allen, executive assistant to the president, for his great organizational gifts and for helping me to make these writing projects a protected priority.

In the end, I especially want to express my heartfelt gratitude to my wife, Mary, and to our children, Katie and Christopher. Their support is invaluable, their wisdom is priceless, their love is so freely given, and their ability to humble their husband and father is beyond doubt. It also helps that they make me laugh.

PREFACE

Has God disappeared? The tragic reality is that we are living in an age that is marked by so much spiritual and theological confusion that the God of the Bible has largely disappeared from view—replaced by less imposing deities that are more amenable to the modern mind.

In one sense, we are witnessing the result of secularization and the evaporation of biblical theism from our public life. To this we must add the privatization of truth and the fact that millions of Americans claim a divine right to their own spiritual cocoon and belief system. As the song suggests, Americans now lay claim to their "own personal Jesus." This personal vision of Jesus Christ may well bear little or no resemblance to Jesus as He is revealed in the Bible.

Indeed, the abdication of biblical faith is one of the hallmarks of our age—whether you prefer to call it postmodern, hypermodern, or post-postmodern. Yet, once the faith is severed from biblical authority, Christianity becomes essentially plastic; a malleable and changeable belief system that just begs for transformation into some other shape and substance.

The situation is complicated further by the embrace of an "openness" that is not open to authentic biblical Christianity. *Tolerance* becomes a code word for avoiding truth, and *openness* means never having to make a judgment about truth at all.

A rescue from this predicament would appear more hopeful but for the fact that the church has, in large part, apparently joined the revolution. Theological fads and fashions dot the American religious landscape, and far too many Christian churches flirt with doctrinal disaster.

As always, truth is the essential issue. Where a clear notion of truth is absent, Christianity becomes more of an attitude than a belief system. But belief has always stood at the center of Christianity, and belief presupposes a truth that can and must be known.

The issues addressed within this book are matters of continuing concern within the Christian church. Intelligent and faithful Christians should know of these issues, and this book is intended to help believers to understand what is at stake.

In the end, the hope for the church is the hope of our lives—Jesus Christ. As our Lord promised, the gates of hell shall not prevail over His church. This is a promise we can trust, even (and especially) in the face of current controversies and concerns.

God has certainly *not* disappeared, but the belief that He has sets our present challenge squarely before us. We will soon find out whether this generation of Christians is up to the challenge.

A CALL FOR
THEOLOGICAL TRIAGE

In every generation, the church is commanded to "contend for the faith that was once for all delivered to the saints." That is no easy task, and it is complicated by the multiple attacks upon Christian truth that mark our contemporary age. Assaults upon the Christian faith are no longer directed only at isolated doctrines. The entire structure of Christian truth is now under attack by those who would subvert Christianity's theological integrity.

Today's Christian faces the daunting task of strategizing which Christian doctrines and theological issues are to be given highest priority in terms of our contemporary context. This applies both to the public defense of Christianity in the face of the secular challenge and the internal responsibility of dealing with doctrinal disagreements. Neither is an easy task, but theological seriousness and maturity demand that we consider doctrinal issues in terms of their relative importance. God's truth is to be defended at every point and in every detail, but responsible Christians must determine which issues deserve first-rank attention in a time of theological crisis.

A trip to the local hospital emergency room some years ago alerted me to an intellectual tool that is most helpful in fulfilling our theological responsibility. In recent years, emergency medical personnel have practiced a discipline known as triage—a process that allows trained personnel to make a quick evaluation of relative medical urgency. Given the chaos of an emergency room reception area, someone must be armed with the medical expertise to make an immediate determination of medical priority. Which patients should be rushed into surgery? Which patients can wait for a less urgent examination? Medical personnel cannot flinch from asking these questions and from taking responsibility to give the patients with the most critical needs top priority in terms of treatment.

The word *triage* comes from the French word *trier,* which means "to sort." Thus, the triage officer in the medical context is the front-line agent for deciding which patients need the most urgent treatment. Without such a process, the scraped knee would receive the same urgency of consideration as a gunshot wound to the chest. The same discipline that brings order to the hectic arena of the emergency room can also offer great assistance to Christians defending truth in the present age.

A discipline of theological triage would require Christians to determine a scale of theological urgency that would correspond to the medical world's framework for medical priority. With this in mind, I would suggest three different levels of theological urgency, each corresponding to a set of issues and theological priorities found in current doctrinal debates.

First-level theological issues would include those doctrines most central and essential to the Christian faith. Included among these most crucial doctrines would be doctrines such as the Trinity, the full deity and humanity of Jesus Christ, justification by faith, and the authority of Scripture.

In the earliest centuries of the Christian movement, heretics directed their most dangerous attacks upon the church's understanding of who Jesus is, and in what sense He is the very Son of God. Other crucial debates concerned the question of how the Son is related to the Father and the Holy Spirit. The earliest creeds and councils of the church were, in essence, emergency measures taken to protect the central core of Christian doctrine. At historic turning points such as the councils at Nicaea, Constantinople, and Chalcedon, orthodoxy was vindicated and heresy was condemned—and these councils dealt with doctrines of unquestionable first-order importance. Christianity stands or falls on the affirmation that Jesus Christ is fully man and fully God.

The church quickly moved to affirm that both the full deity and full humanity of Jesus Christ are absolutely necessary to the Christian faith. Any denial of what has become known as Nicaean-Chalcedonian Christology is, by definition, condemned as a heresy. The essential truths of the incarnation include the death, burial, and bodily resurrection of the Lord Jesus Christ. Those who deny these revealed truths are, by definition, not Christians.

The same is true with the doctrine of the Trinity. The early church clarified and codified its understanding of the one true and living God by affirming the full deity of the Father, the Son, and the Holy Spirit—while insisting that the Bible reveals one God in three persons.

In addition to the Christological and Trinitarian doctrines, the doctrine of justification by faith must also be included among these first-order truths. Without this doctrine, we are left with a denial of the gospel itself, and salvation is transformed into some structure of human righteousness. The truthfulness and authority of the Holy Scriptures must also rank as a first-order doctrine, for without an affirmation of the Bible as the very Word of God, we are left without any adequate authority for distinguishing truth from error.

These first-order doctrines represent the most fundamental truths of the Christian faith, and a denial of these doctrines represents nothing less than an eventual denial of Christianity itself.

The set of second-order doctrines is distinguished from the first-order set by the fact that believing Christians may disagree on the second-order issues, though this disagreement will create significant boundaries between believers. When Christians organize themselves into congregations and denominational forms, these boundaries become evident.

Second-order issues would include the meaning and mode of baptism. Baptists and Presbyterians, for example, fervently disagree over the most basic understanding of Christian baptism. The practice of infant baptism is inconceivable to the Baptist mind, while Presbyterians trace infant baptism to their most basic understanding of the covenant. Standing together on the first-order doctrines, Baptists and Presbyterians eagerly recognize each other as believing Christians, but recognize that disagreement on issues of this importance will prevent fellowship within the same congregation or denomination.

Christians across a vast denominational range can

stand together on the first-order doctrines and recognize each other as authentic Christians, while understanding that the existence of second-order disagreements prevents the closeness of fellowship we would otherwise enjoy. A church either will recognize infant baptism, or it will not. That choice immediately creates a second-order conflict with those who take the other position by conviction.

In recent years, the issue of women serving as pastors has emerged as another second-order issue. Again, a church or denomination either will ordain women to the pastorate, or it will not. Second-order issues resist easy settlement by those who would prefer an either/or approach. Many of the most heated disagreements among serious believers take place at the second-order level, for these issues frame our understanding of the church and its ordering by the Word of God.

Third-order issues are doctrines over which Christians may disagree and remain in close fellowship, even within local congregations. I would put most of the debates over eschatology, for example, in this category. Christians who affirm the bodily, historical, and victorious return of the Lord Jesus Christ may differ over timetable and sequence without rupturing the fellowship of the church. Christians may find themselves in disagreement over any number of issues related to the interpretation of difficult texts or the understanding of matters of common disagreement. Nevertheless, standing together on issues of more urgent importance, believers are able to accept one another without compromise when third-order issues are in question.

A structure of theological triage does not imply that Christians may take any biblical truth with less than full seriousness. We are charged to embrace and to teach the comprehensive truthfulness of the Christian faith as revealed in the Holy Scriptures. There are no insignificant doctrines revealed in the Bible, but there is an essential foundation of truth that undergirds the entire system of biblical truth.

This structure of theological triage may also help to explain how confusion can often occur in the midst of doctrinal debate. If the relative urgency of these truths is not taken into account, the debate can quickly become unhelpful. The error of theological liberalism is evident in a basic disrespect for biblical authority and the church's treasury of truth. The mark of true liberalism is the refusal to admit that first-order theological issues even exist. Liberals treat first-order doctrines as if they were merely third-order in importance, and doctrinal ambiguity is the inevitable result.

Fundamentalism, on the other hand, tends toward

the opposite error. The misjudgment of true fundamentalism is the belief that all disagreements concern first-order doctrines. Thus, third-order issues are raised to a first-order importance, and Christians are wrongly and harmfully divided.

Living in an age of widespread doctrinal denial and intense theological confusion, thinking Christians must rise to the challenge of Christian maturity, even in the midst of a theological emergency. We must sort the issues with a trained mind and a humble heart, in order to protect what the apostle Paul called the "treasure" that has been entrusted to us. Given the urgency of this challenge, a lesson from the emergency room just might help.

2

GUARDED THROUGH FAITH

Assurance and the Doctrine of Perseverance

Traumatic world events and nagging questions of belief sometimes cause Christians to be troubled in spirit and to question their assurance of faith. In every generation, believers have struggled with the question of assurance in salvation. As always, the church confronts this issue as both a pressing theological question and as an urgent pastoral concern. Answering these questions anew, we are reminded once again that all doctrine is practical and that the great biblical truths of the Christian faith are meant not only for our intellectual acceptance, but also for our spiritual health.

Many Christians suffer from an absence of Christian assurance. They lack confidence in their salvation and are troubled by nagging doubts, perplexing questions, and a lack of clarity about whether assurance of salvation is actually possible. At the same time, the church has always faced the reality of false professors and those who fall away. These are problems that trouble the soul and raise unavoidable theological questions.

Clearly, now is the time for clarification and for the recovery of a biblical concept of assurance. Beyond the immediate questions of assurance and false professors, the church must also confront superficial and inadequate understandings of assurance—concepts that can actually mislead and confuse.

The apostle Paul assured the Christians in Philippi of his absolute confidence "that he who began a good work in you will bring it to completion at the day of Jesus Christ" (Philippians 1:6, ESV). The logic of that passage is of vital importance. Paul's confidence was not that the Philippians would be able to preserve *themselves*. To the contrary, Paul's confidence was established in Jesus Christ and in the promise that Christ would complete the work He had surely begun in them.

Coming to the end of his own life, Paul expressed personal confidence that the Lord would "bring me safely to His heavenly kingdom" (2 Timothy 4:18). Without this confidence, how could Paul have faced the prospect of his own death? His desire was for fellow believers to experience this same confidence and assurance.

Jesus taught His disciples a great deal about the believer's assurance, ultimately establishing assurance in the Father's promises to the Son. In the gospel of John, Jesus teaches that "this is the will of him who sent me, that I should lose nothing of all that he has given me, but raise it up on the last day" (John 6:39, ESV). This is a magnificent promise, and one that makes sense only in light of Jesus's straightforward revelation concerning the Father's authority in salvation: "All that the Father gives me will come to me, and whoever comes to me I will never cast out" (John 6:37, ESV). Those who are in Christ's hands will never be lost, for they have been called, drawn, and given to Him by the Father Himself. As Jesus the Good Shepherd said in John 10, "My sheep hear my voice, and I know them, and they follow me. I give them eternal life, and they will never perish, and no one will snatch them out of my hand. My Father, who has given them to me, is greater than all, and no one is able to snatch them out of the Father's hand" (John 10:27–29, ESV).

Thus a consistent biblical theme emerges from the scriptural text. Jesus assured His disciples that their salvation was rooted in the eternal purposes of God and that those who truly come to faith in Him are safe within

God's mercy. No one is able to snatch believers out of the Father's hand, and all who come to the Son are preserved by the Father.

Christians should find great comfort in the biblical promises of assurance. This is because these promises are founded ultimately in the eternal purposes of God, in the Son's accomplished work, and in the Father's vindication of the Son. Those who truly come to Christ by faith are guarded, preserved, and kept by the power of God. Our Lord did not intend His people to be trapped in a maze of doubt and insecurity. To the contrary, Christ instructed His sheep to trust in Him and His promises.

Assurance of salvation is indeed possible—and is a Christian responsibility. Pernicious doubt concerning salvation may be an indication that the believer does not truly trust the character, power, and purposes of God. Thus a believer's insecurity—sometimes disguised as an artificial humility—can be evidence of a heart that does not adequately trust in the promises of God.

At the same time, saving faith is demonstrated in a transformed life. Peter, for example, instructed believers to observe their lives, looking for the evidence of authentic faith and the marks of true discipleship. Peter summarized his exhortation with these unforgettable words: "Therefore, brothers, be all the more diligent to make your calling and election sure, for if you practice these qualities you will never fall" (2 Peter 1:10, ESV).

How are believers to make their "calling and election sure"? There can be no question that Peter expected Christians to look and strive for the characteristics that should mark those who have been transformed by the power of God. Thus, the believer's calling and election—the very foundation of the salvation experience—would be evident in a new heart and a transformed life.

Paul also repeatedly warned Christians not to abandon their faith or to fall prey to false teachers. He even went so far as to identify some who had "nullified" the grace of God (Galatians 2:21) and others who had fallen away and abandoned their faith. Demas, for example, who "loved this present world," had deserted Paul and the gospel (2 Timothy 4:10). Hymanaeus and Alexander had "suffered shipwreck in regard to their faith" and thus had been handed over to Satan by Paul "that they will be taught not to blaspheme" (1 Timothy 1:20).

In pondering biblical warnings like these, most Christians think of the passages in Hebrews that have spawned so many different interpretations. How are we to understand these warnings—particularly as found in Hebrews 6:4–8? No doubt this is a crucial question, for how we interpret this passage is inextricably tied to larger theological issues—including our understanding of the church itself.

The warnings of Hebrews 6 are seen in the clearest light when put alongside Jesus's parable of the sower and the soils, as found in Matthew 13 and Luke 8. Comparing the human heart to soils of the field, Jesus pointed to the reality that the church would encounter those who would "believe for a while" but would fall away under testing or persecution. When Jesus identified the shallow soil, He was certainly speaking of those whose faith would be, as described by the Puritans, a *temporary* or false faith. Thus, those who are described as falling away in Hebrews 6 are those who falsely confessed faith in Christ. As with the soil that bore fruit for a time but withered, so with those who have "tasted the heavenly gift" but fall away. Theirs was not a genuine and enduring faith, but a fickle and false faith. This is an urgent and sober warning.

In the final analysis, the gift of assurance rests on the biblical doctrine of perseverance. This doctrine teaches that true believers are those who persevere in and by faith. Their endurance—having been preserved by the power of God—becomes the demonstration of their salvation and the mark of authenticity. The biblical doctrine of perseverance corrects misunderstandings implied by more superficial conceptions of the believer's state. Some teach that anyone who has at any time made a profession of faith in Christ or exercised the slightest belief is secure. These teachers actually argue that true believers may demonstrate absolutely *none* of the marks of gospel authenticity. In other words, such persons never repent of their sins—and may even repudiate the faith—but are supposed to be secure in their salvation. Nothing could be further from the truth.

Furthermore, the doctrine of perseverance harmoniously links the believer's assurance of salvation to the larger scheme of redemption. God's determination to save sinners is affirmed from beginning to end. The believer's faith in Christ, exercised as an act of the believer's will, is understood to be itself a gift of God and a result of God's calling. Thus the doctrine of perseverance grounds assurance in the eternal purposes of God, by which God determines to redeem His people through the cross of the Lord Jesus Christ, and to preserve Christ's church throughout all the ages.

In his first letter, Peter reminded Christians that the Father "has caused us to be born again to a living hope through the resurrection of Jesus Christ from the dead." Believers are promised "an inheritance which is imperishable and undefiled and will not fade away, reserved in heaven for you, who are protected by the power of God through faith for a salvation ready to be revealed in the last time" (1 Peter 1:3–5). The Christian's proper assurance of salvation is God's gift—a gift given to the believer by the very God who has accomplished our salvation. True believers are those who have genuinely responded to the call of the gospel, whose belief is evident in a life transformed by God's grace, and whose profession of faith in Christ is accompanied by repentance from sin and an eagerness to follow Christ.

Believers do sin, and may sin grievously, but they can never finally remain in sin. Peter promised that God will guard His own through faith, even as salvation will be revealed "in the last time." In the end, the gift of assurance and the doctrine of perseverance take us back to the very essence of the gospel—we are saved by grace through faith. Grace alone…nothing more and nothing less.

3

CAN WE BE GOOD
WITHOUT GOD?

The greatest moral question hanging over America's increasingly secular culture is this: Can we be good without God? That vital question—though almost always unasked—is the backdrop for most of the issues aflame in the media, the schools, and the courts.

Secularization, the process by which a society severs its ties to a religious worldview, is now pressed to the limits by ideological secularists bent on removing all vestiges of the Judeo-Christian heritage from the nation's culture. They will not stop until every aspect of Christian morality is supplanted by the new morality of the postmodern philosophers—a morality with no absolutes, and without God.

How bad is it? Harvard law professor Alan Dershowitz, an influential liberal partisan in the culture wars, rejects the idea that belief in God is necessary for moral goodness. In *Letters to a Young Lawyer,* Dershowitz argues that obedience to the God of the Bible can often be immoral. We should not be good because we fear divine punishment, Dershowitz argues, but because we aspire to good character. "In deciding what course of action is moral," he instructs, "you should act as if there were no God. You should also act as if there were no threat of earthly punishment or reward. You should be a person of good character because it is right to be such a person."[1]

Of course, this begs the question of character itself. How do we know what character is without an objective reference? If human beings are left to our own devices and limited to our own wisdom, we will invent whatever model of "good character" seems right at the time. Without God there are no moral absolutes. Without moral absolutes, there is no authentic knowledge of right and wrong.

According to the new American secular orthodoxy, no reference to God or faith—no matter how vague or distant—is allowable in public conversation, much less in governmental policy making. The end result is a total col-

1. Alan Dershowitz, *Letters to a Young Lawyer* (New York: Basic Books, 2001), 199.

lapse of moral conversation. All that is left is a burlesque of moral nonsense with endless debates going nowhere in particular, except away from Christianity.

For example, we are now told that concern for sexual abstinence is just another imposition of a Christian morality. Planned Parenthood and the proponents of teenage sexual activity oppose abstinence-based sex education as "inherently religious."[2] That is, the only arguments against teenage sexual promiscuity are based on religious convictions—which are forbidden grounds for public consideration.

In fact, the American Civil Liberties Union has successfully fought abstinence-based programs in several states, arguing that such programs violate their radical notion of church/state separation, and put the public schools in the position of teaching "religion."

This nonsense would be laughable if its results were not so devastating among America's young people. One parent opposed the program, stating: "I am extremely upset that this school board wants to teach my Jewish kids Christian values." Pardon me, but who dropped Judaism from the Judeo-Christian heritage? Christianity

---

2. www.nytimes.com/2005/12/08/fashion/thursdaystyles/08purity.html? pagewanted=print.

and Judaism differ on any number of central issues of faith, but we share the Ten Commandments. As Rabbi Jacob Neusner once lamented: "A country without a sense of shame or of sin does not have a sense of what is right or wrong, just what is useful or what you can get away with or not get away with."

Are moral values now off-limits just because they may be affirmed or shared by Christians? As columnist Mona Charen asked, "Have we reached the point in America where virtue is considered contaminated because it has been known to keep company with religion?"

If abstinence-based sex education is "inherently religious," then so is the criminal code that outlaws murder. After all, "Thou shalt not kill" was first inscribed on tablets of stone by God, not contrived by a secularist lawmaker in Washington. What about prohibitions against robbery, rape, or lying? Out with them all, for they are part of God's moral law as well.

The sheer nonsense of this makes it difficult to take the argument seriously, but courts at the local, state, and federal levels are heeding these secularist arguments. Our ability to conduct any meaningful moral discourse is fast evaporating.

Just how far we have come is made clear by a glance at the most formative legal commentary that lies behind this nation's legal tradition, William Blackstone's *Commentaries on the Laws of England.* English common law is, after all, the basis of our own legal doctrines. Just before the American Revolution, Blackstone wrote: "Man, considered as a creature, must necessarily be subject to the laws of his Creator, for he is entirely a dependant being."[3]

The legal tradition that gave birth to this nation, formed the background of its constitution, and sustained our laws and their interpretation for a century and a half is now itself ruled out-of-bounds. Any moral tradition that even whispers the memory of the Almighty is now ruled null and void.

But can Americans be good without God? Can we even entertain the fiction that citizens can create a totally secular morality? Nonsense. There is no secular morality of any substance. As Fyodor Dostoyevsky acknowledged, "If God is dead, everything is permissible."

So, we live among the ruins of a moral value structure destroyed by the wrecking ball of a radical secularist agenda, but already weakened by compromise from within—even from within the church.

The Church of England and its sister church in

---

3. William Blackstone, *Commentaries on the Laws of England,* vol. 1 (1769; repr., Chicago: University of Chicago Press, 1979), 39.

America, the Episcopal Church (USA), are competing in a disbelief derby to see which church can produce more heretical bishops. Richard Holloway, Anglican bishop of Edinburgh, now argues that morality must be freed from Christian teaching for the modern age. As he argues:

> We either admit that God is, to some extent at least, a human construct that is subject to criticism and evolution, or we weld religion to unsustainable prejudices that guarantee its rejection for the best, not the worst of reasons, so that to abandon it becomes a virtuous act of revolt against an oppressive force that imprisons rather than liberates humanity.[4]

According to this bishop, the only way to be moral is to reject the Bible and the very notion of moral absolutes. In effect, the only way to be a good person is to function as an atheist.

With Friedrich Nietzsche, Holloway wants modern humanity to be freed from "slave obedience" to the morality of the Bible. In *Godless Morality*, the bishop insists that we must just learn to live with moral ambigu-

---

4. Richard Holloway, *Godless Morality: Keeping Religion Out of Ethics* (Edinburgh: Canongate Books, 1999), 4.

ity. As for Scripture, it must be abandoned as authoritative moral guidance, for "it no longer conforms to our experience of truth and value."[5]

The same rejection of biblical morality is all too common on these shores as well. Liberal theologians and church leaders display the same embarrassment over the moral teachings of the Bible. Among evangelicals, outright rejection of biblical authority is more rare (at least for now), but too many pulpits remain empty of biblical content and moral confrontation with the issues of the day.

In the confused public square of America's cultural currents, the situation is far worse. Now that God is off-limits, we face the morality of the cultural elites and media celebrities.

Evidence of the inevitable confusion that results was seen in the nation's nonsensical moral fireworks over Michael Jackson's arrest for child molestation. Americans seemed certain that Jackson's publicly acknowledged behavior—much less his alleged crime—was wrong, even immoral. But why? Did his trial for sexual molestation bring moral clarity to the situation? Probably not. Lawyers like Alan Dershowitz earn their lavish incomes by making certain that moral arguments are kept out of the picture. As Dershowitz instructs young lawyers, "So

5. Holloway, *Godless Morality*, 81.

you want to do good. Don't we all? But when you become a lawyer, you have to define good differently than you did before."[6] Obviously.

Some years ago, a group of boys at Lakewood High School in southern California were arrested as members of a "sexual posse" that kept score at the sport of sexual intercourse with different girls. Several of the boys' fathers said that nothing was wrong with their behavior. One of the Lakewood boys, said, "They pass out condoms, teach sex education and pregnancy...but they don't teach us any rules."[7]

Welcome to post-Christian America. All the rules are off—it's everyone for himself. Write your own rules, find your own way, just be sure to leave God out of it. The apostle Paul wrote to the church at Rome, warning that "the wrath of God is revealed from heaven against all ungodliness and unrighteousness of men who suppress the truth in unrighteousness, because that which is known about God is evident within them; for God made it evident to them" (Romans 1:18–19). God is not mocked. Welcome to Rome—America in the postmodern age.

6. Dershowitz, *Letters to a Young Lawyer,* 41.

7. "Scoring With the Spur Posse," *New York Times,* March 30, 1993.

4

THE DISAPPEARANCE OF SIN

A Flight from Reality

The disappearance of *sin* from our moral vocabulary is one of the hallmarks of the modern age—and of postmodern morality. These days, most people think themselves to be imperfect, leaving room for improvement—but they do not think of themselves as sinners in need of forgiveness and redemption. This point has been raised by many, but an early prophet of sin's disappearance was not a theologian but a psychiatrist.

Karl Menninger, a famous American psychiatrist, was among the first mental heath professionals to suggest that some psychological disorders were actually treatable.

The established thought at the time was that virtually all mental disorders were incurable, but Menninger was unwilling to accept that assumption. His innovative treatment of psychological diseases largely shaped the modern practice of psychiatry.

Nevertheless, Menninger was not without controversy. Perhaps his most controversial contribution came in the form of his 1973 book, *Whatever Became of Sin?* The psychological community had almost universally banned the word *sin* from its vocabulary. In fact, therapists blamed the notion of sin for producing guilt, which seemed to be psychologically unhealthy. How's that for a reversal of reality?

Menninger wrote with moral indignation. He understood the reason the notion of sin had been rejected by psychiatry, but he found that he could not explain all human behavior as either "neurotic" or "healthy." There was another category of behavior, as Menninger observed—and that category was sin. Menninger's book was a powerful and influential call for recognizing sin as sin. He demonstrated that the psychological community was not alone; society at large had rejected the notion of sin.

Words such as *disease, antisocial behavior,* and *lack of moral development* had replaced *sin* as explanations for human behavior. Menninger attacked this evasion.

He wrote: "I believe there is 'sin' which is expressed in ways which cannot be subsumed…as 'crime,' 'disease,' 'delinquency,' 'deviancy.' There *is* immorality; there *is* unethical behavior; there *is* wrongdoing. And I hope to show that there is usefulness in retaining the concept, and indeed the word, SIN, which now shows some signs of returning to public acceptance."[1]

Menninger's call was heard by some of his fellow psychologists but rejected by many. His recovery of "sin" was seen by many of his colleagues as a giant step backward for a progressive science. Furthermore, his hope that sin might return as a public concern was not realized.

Genuine Christianity cannot escape dealing with sin. The gospel will not allow any evasion of sin as the universal human condition of revolt against the Creator, the God of absolute holiness and absolute love. Nevertheless, Menninger's question still remains an indictment of the church as well as society: Whatever became of sin?

The famous psychiatrist noted the absence of "sin" in his profession, but we should notice the decline of "sin" within the church. Some leading churches and television preachers have followed the lead of the psychological community in rejecting the notion of sin. The word

---

1. Karl Menninger, *Whatever Became of Sin?* (New York: Hawthorn Books, 1973), 46.

is seldom uttered in many churches—even some who would describe themselves as evangelical.

This is an abdication of the gospel. Where sin is not faced as sin, grace cannot be grace. What need have men and women of atonement when they are told that their deepest problem is something less than what the Bible explicitly teaches? Weak teaching on sin leads to cheap grace, and neither leads to the gospel.

Scripture identifies sin as humanity's willful revolt against God. It is rebellion and disobedience. Furthermore, it is "missing the mark" of faithfulness to God's holy standard. It is the most fundamental human problem, and it is the reason we need a Savior. It is a revolt against God's authority and an insult to God's glory. It is humanity in moral revolt, usually disguised as personal autonomy.

Christians have had a hard time striking a biblical balance. Some minimalize sin so that it seems not to apply to their behavior. Others may fixate on certain "pet" sins as their only concern and neglect the more pressing commands. Some churches deal with sin but never get to the gospel. Liberal denominations have abandoned the biblical doctrine of sin and now locate sin only in the structures of society. None of these perversions is worthy of the gospel.

Whatever became of sin? It has been redefined, ignored, rejected, neglected, and denied. Yet human beings know of its reality. Those who deny its reality were once described by another psychiatrist as "People of the Lie."[2]

The church must be the people of the truth. Though society and popular culture may reject sin as unsophisticated and outdated, the church must speak the word of truth. Therapy has its rightful place, and Christians should not disparage the legitimate use of psychological insights. Christian psychologists and psychiatrists should serve, in the truest sense, as healing ministers. Nevertheless, the Christian knows that the most fundamental problem faced by humanity cannot be overcome by therapy but only by atonement. And that is the gospel truth.

2. M. Scott Peck, *People of the Lie* (New York: Touchstone, 1998).

5

HELL UNDER FIRE, PART 1

After reviewing the rise of the modern age, the Italian literary critic Piero Camporesi commented, "We can now affirm…that hell is finished, that the great theatre of torments is closed for an indeterminate period, and that after almost 2,000 years of horrifying performances the play will not be repeated. The long, triumphal season has come to an end."[1] Like a play with a good run, the curtain has finally come down, and for millions around the world the biblical doctrine of hell is but a distant memory. For so many persons in this postmodern world, the biblical doctrine of hell has become simply unthinkable.

---

1. Piero Camporesi, *The Fear of Hell: Images of Damnation and Salvation in Early Modern Europe,* trans. Lucinda Byatt (University Park, PA: Pennsylvania State University Press, 1991), vi.

Have postmodern Westerners just decided that hell is no more? Can we really just think the doctrine away? Os Guinness notes that Western societies "have reached the stage in pluralization where choice is not just a state of affairs, it is a state of mind. Choice has become a value in itself, even a priority. To be modern is to be addicted to choice and change. Change becomes the very essence of life."[2] Personal choice becomes the urgency; what sociologist Peter Berger called the "heretical imperative."[3] In such a context, theology undergoes rapid and repeated transformation driven by cultural currents. For millions of persons in the postmodern age, truth is a matter of personal choice—not divine revelation. Clearly, we moderns do not choose for hell to exist.

This process of change is often invisible to those experiencing it, and denied by those promoting it. As David F. Wells comments, "The stream of historic orthodoxy that once watered the evangelical soul is now dammed by a worldliness that many fail to recognize as worldliness because of the cultural innocence with which it presents itself." He continues:

2. Os Guinness, *The Gravedigger File: Papers on the Subversion of the Modern Church* (Downers Grove, IL: InterVarsity Press, 1983), 96.

3. Peter L. Berger, *The Heretical Imperative: Contemporary Possibilities of Religious Affirmation* (Garden City, NY: Doubleday, 1979).

To be sure, this orthodoxy never was infallible, nor was it without its blemishes and foibles, but I am far from persuaded that the emancipation from its theological core that much of evangelicalism is effecting has resulted in greater biblical fidelity. In fact, the result is just the opposite. We now have less biblical fidelity, less interest in truth, less seriousness, less depth, and less capacity to speak the Word of God to our own generation in a way that offers an alternative to what it already thinks.[4]

The pressing question of our concern is this: Whatever happened to hell? What has happened so that we now find even some who claim to be evangelicals promoting and teaching concepts such as universalism, inclusivism, postmortem evangelism, conditional immortality, and annihilationism—when those known as evangelicals in former times were known for opposing those very proposals? Many evangelicals seek to find any way out of the biblical doctrine—marked by so much awkwardness and embarrassment.

The answer to these questions must be found in

---

4. David F. Wells, *No Place for Truth: Or Whatever Happened to Evangelical Theology?* (Grand Rapids: Eerdmans, 1993), 11–12.

understanding the impact of cultural trends and the prevailing worldview upon Christian theology. Ever since the Enlightenment, theologians have been forced to defend the very legitimacy of their discipline and proposals. A secular worldview that denies supernatural revelation must reject Christianity as a system and truth-claim. At the same time, it seeks to transform all religious truth-claims into matters of personal choice and opinion. Christianity, stripped of its offensive theology, is reduced to one "spirituality" among others.

All the same, there are particular doctrines that are especially odious and repulsive to the modern and postmodern mind. The traditional doctrine of hell as a place of everlasting punishment bears that scandal in a particular way. The doctrine is offensive to modern sensibilities and an embarrassment to many who consider themselves to be Christians. Those Friedrich Schleiermacher called the "cultured despisers of religion" especially despise the doctrine of hell.[5] As one observer has quipped, hell must be air-conditioned.

Liberal Protestantism and Roman Catholicism have modified their theological systems to remove this offense. No one is in danger of hearing a threatening "fire and

---

5. Friedrich Schleiermacher, *On Religion: Speeches to Its Cultured Despisers*, trans. John Oman (New York: Harper and Brothers, 1958).

brimstone" sermon in those churches. The burden of defending and debating hell now falls to the evangelicals—the last people who think it matters.

How is it that so many evangelicals—including some of the most respected leaders in the movement—now reject the traditional doctrine of hell in favor of annihilationism or some other option? The answer must surely come down to the challenge of theodicy—the challenge to defend God's goodness against modern indictments.

Modern secularism demands that anyone who would speak for God must now defend Him. The challenge of theodicy is primarily to defend God against the problem of evil. The societies that gave birth to the decades of megadeath, the Holocaust, the abortion explosion, and institutionalized terror will now demand that God answer their questions and redefine Himself according to their dictates.

In the background of all this is a series of interrelated cultural, theological, and philosophical changes that point to an answer for our question: What happened to evangelical convictions about hell?

The first issue is a changed view of God. The biblical vision of God has been rejected by the culture as too restrictive of human freedom and offensive to human sensibilities. God's love has been redefined so that it is no longer holy. God's sovereignty has been reconceived so that human autonomy is undisturbed. In recent years, even God's omniscience has been redefined to mean that God perfectly knows all that He can perfectly know, but He cannot possibly know a future based on free human decisions.

Evangelical revisionists promote an understanding of divine love that is never coercive and would disallow any thought that God would send impenitent sinners to eternal punishment in the fires of hell. They are seeking to rescue God from the bad reputation He picked up by associating with theologians who for centuries taught the traditional doctrine. God is just not like that, they reassure. He would never sentence anyone—however guilty—to eternal torment and anguish.

Theologian Geerhardus Vos warned against abstracting the love of God from His other attributes, noting that while God's love is revealed to be His fundamental attribute, it is defined by His other attributes as well. It is quite possible to "overemphasize this one side of truth and duty as to bring into neglect other exceedingly important principles and demands of Christianity," he stressed.[6] This would lead to a loss of theological "equilibrium" and bal-

---

6. Geerhardus Vos, "The Scriptural Doctrine of the Love of God," in *Redemptive History and Biblical Interpretation: The Shorter Writings of Geerhardus Vos,* ed. Richard B. Gaffin Jr. (Phillipsburg, NJ: P & R, 1980), 426.

ance. In the specific case of the love of God, it often leads to an unscriptural sentimentalism whereby God's love becomes a form of indulgence incompatible with His hatred of sin.

In this regard, the language of the revisionists is particularly instructive. Any God who would act as the traditional doctrine would hold would be "vindictive," "cruel," and "more like Satan than like God." Clark Pinnock has made the credibility of the doctrine of God to the modern mind a central focus of his theology: "I believe that unless the portrait of God is compelling, the credibility of belief in God is bound to decline." Later, he suggests, "Today it is easier to invite people to find fulfillment in a dynamic, personal God than it would be to ask them to find it in a deity who is immutable and self-enclosed."[7]

Extending this argument further, it would surely be easier to persuade secular persons to believe in a God who would never judge anyone deserving of eternal punishment than it would to persuade them to believe in the God preached by Jonathan Edwards or Charles Spurgeon. But the urgent question is this: Is evangelical theology about marketing God to our contemporary culture,

---

7. Clark H. Pinnock, "Systematic Theology," in *The Openness of God: A Biblical Challenge to the Traditional Understanding of God* (Downers Grove, IL: InterVarsity Press, 1994), 101, 107.

or is it our task to stand in continuity with orthodox biblical conviction—whatever the cost? As was cited earlier, modern persons demand that God must be a humanitarian, and He is held to human standards of righteousness and love. In the end, only God can defend Himself against His critics.

Our responsibility is to present the truth of the Christian faith with boldness, clarity, and courage—and defending the biblical doctrine in these times will require all three of these virtues. Hell is an assured reality, just as it is presented so clearly in the Bible. To run from this truth, to reduce the sting of sin and the threat of hell, is to pervert the gospel and to feed on lies. Hell is not up for a vote or open for revision. Will we surrender this truth to modern skeptics?

6

HELL UNDER FIRE, PART 2

The doctrine of hell has recently come under vicious attack, both from secularists and even from some evangelicals. In many ways, the assault has been a covert one. Like a slowly encroaching tide, a whole complex of interrelated cultural, theological, and philosophical changes have conspired to undermine the traditional understanding of hell. In the last chapter, we considered the first and perhaps most important of those changes—a radically altered view of God. But other issues have played a part as well.

A second issue that has contributed to the modern denial of hell is a changed view of justice. Retributive justice has been the hallmark of human law since premodern times.

This concept assumes that punishment is a natural and necessary component of justice. Nevertheless, retributive justice has been under assault for many years in Western cultures, and this has led to modifications in the doctrine of hell.

Utilitarian philosophers such as John Stuart Mill and Jeremy Bentham argued that retribution is an unacceptable form of justice. Rejecting clear and absolute moral norms, they argued that justice demands restoration rather than retribution. Criminals were no longer seen as evil and deserving of punishment, but were seen as persons in need of correction. The goal—for all but the most egregious sinners—was restoration and rehabilitation. The shift from the prison to the penitentiary was supposed to be a shift from a place of punishment to a place of penance, but apparently no one told the prisoners.

C. S. Lewis rejected this idea as an assault upon the very concept of justice. "We demand of a cure not whether it is just but whether it succeeds. Thus when we cease to consider what the criminal deserves and consider only what will cure him or deter others, we have tacitly removed him from the sphere of justice altogether; instead of a person, a subject of rights, we now have a mere object, a patient, a 'case.' "[1]

Penal reforms followed, public executions ceased, and

---

1. C. S. Lewis, "The Humanitarian Theory of Punishment" in *God in the Dock: Essays on Theology and Ethics,* ed. Walter Hooper (Grand Rapids: Eerdmans, 1970), 288.

the public accepted the changes in the name of humanitarianism. Dutch criminologist Pieter Spierenburg pointed to "increasing inter-human identification" as the undercurrent of this shift.[2] Individuals began to sympathize with the criminal, often thinking of themselves in the criminal's place. The impact of this shift in the culture is apparent in a letter from one nineteenth-century Anglican to another:

> The disbelief in the existence of retributive justice…is now so widely spread through nearly all classes of people, especially in regard to social and political questions…[that it] causes even men, whose theology teaches them to look upon God as a vindictive, lawless autocrat, to stigmatize as cruel and heathenish the belief that criminal law is bound to contemplate in punishment other ends beside the improvement of the offender himself and the deterring of others.[3]

---

2. Pieter Spierenburg, *The Spectacle of Suffering: Executions and the Evolution of Repression* (Cambridge: Cambridge University Press, 1984), cited in Kendall S. Harmon, "Finally Excluded from God? Some Twentieth Century Theological Explorations of the Problem of Hell and Universalism with Reference to the Historical Development of These Doctrines" (D. Phil. Thesis, Oxford University, 1993), 110.

3. Letter from Fenton J. A. Hort to F. D. Maurice dated November 16, 1849, cited in Harmon, 112.

The utilitarian concept of justice and deterrence has also given way to justice by popular opinion and cultural custom. The U.S. Constitution disallows "cruel and unusual punishment," and the courts have offered evolving and conflicting rulings on what kind of punishment is thus excluded. At various times the death penalty has been constitutionally permitted and forbidden, and in one recent U.S. Supreme Court decision, the justice writing the majority opinion actually cited data from opinion polls.

The transformations of legal practice and culture have redefined justice for many modern persons. Retribution is out, and rehabilitation is put in its place. Some theologians have simply incorporated this new theory of justice into their doctrines of hell. For the Roman Catholics, the doctrine of purgatory functions as the penitentiary. For some evangelicals, a period of time in hell—but not an eternity in hell—is the remedy.

Some theologians have questioned the moral integrity of eternal punishment by arguing that an infinite punishment is an unjust penalty for finite sins. Or, to put the argument in a slightly different form, eternal torment is no fitting punishment for temporal sins. The traditional doctrine of hell argues that an infinite penalty is just punishment for sin against the infinite holiness of

God. This explains why all sinners are equally deserving of hell, but for salvation through faith in Christ.

A third shift in the larger culture concerns the advent of the psychological worldview. Human behavior has been redefined by the impact of humanistic psychologies that deny or reduce personal responsibility for wrong-doing. Various theories place the blame on external influences, biological factors, behavioral determinism, genetic predispositions, and the influence of the subconscious—and these variant theories barely scratch the surface.

The autonomous self becomes the great personal project for individuals, and their various crimes and misdemeanors are excused as growth experiences or "personal issues." Shame and guilt are banned from public discussion and dismissed as repressive. In such a culture, the finality of God's sentencing of impenitent sinners to hell is simply unthinkable.

A fourth shift concerns the concept of salvation. The vast majority of men and women throughout the centuries of Western civilization have awakened in the morning and gone to sleep at night with the fear of hell never far from consciousness—until now. Sin has been redefined as a lack of self-esteem rather than as an insult to the glory of God. Salvation has been reconceived as liberation from oppression, internal or external. The gospel becomes a means of release from bondage to bad habits rather than rescue from a sentence of eternity in hell.

The theodicy issue arises immediately when evangelicals limit salvation to those who come to conscious faith in Christ during their earthly lives and define salvation as anything akin to justification by faith. To the modern mind this seems absolutely unfair and scandalously discriminatory. Some evangelicals have thus modified the doctrine of salvation accordingly. This means that hell is either evacuated or minimized. Or, as one Catholic wit quipped, hell has been air-conditioned.

These shifts in the culture are but part of the picture. The most basic cause of controversy over the doctrine of hell is the challenge of theodicy. The traditional doctrine is just too out of step with the contemporary mind—too harsh and eternally fixed. In virtually every aspect, the modern mind is offended by the biblical concept of hell preserved in the traditional doctrine. For some who call themselves evangelicals, this is simply too much to bear.

We should note that compromise on the doctrine of hell is not limited to those who reject the traditional formulation. The reality is that few references to hell are likely to be heard even in conservative churches that would never deny the doctrine. Once again, the cultural environment is a major influence.

In his study of "seeker sensitive" churches, researcher Kimon Howland Sargeant notes that "today's cultural pluralism fosters an under-emphasis on the 'hard sell' of hell while contributing to an overemphasis on the 'soft sell' of personal satisfaction through Jesus Christ."[4] The problem is thus more complex and pervasive than the theological rejection of hell—it also includes the avoidance of the issue in the face of cultural pressure.

The revision or rejection of the traditional doctrine of hell comes at a great cost. The entire system of theology is modified by effect, even if some revisionists refuse to take their revisions to their logical conclusions. Essentially, our very concepts of God and the gospel are at stake. What could be more important?

The temptation to revise the doctrine of hell—to remove the sting and scandal of everlasting conscious punishment—is understandable. But it is also a major test of evangelical conviction. This is no theological trifle. As one observer has asked, "Could it be that the only result of attempts, however well-meaning, to air-condition Hell, is to ensure that more and more people wind up there?"[5]

---

4. Kimon Howland Sargeant, *Seeker Churches: Promoting Traditional Religion in a Nontraditional Way* (New Brunswick: Rutgers University Press, 2000), 198.

5. "Hell Air-Conditioned," New Oxford Review 58 (June 3 1998), 4.

Hell demands our attention in the present, confronting evangelicals with a critical test of theological and biblical integrity. Hell may be denied, but it will not disappear.

7

A CHRISTIAN VISION OF BEAUTY, PART 1

I would like to bring up the idea of a Christian vision of beauty, but as I do so I am struck by the fact that this discussion is so rare. There are altogether too few opportunities for Christians to ponder some of the biggest questions of life. We tend to focus on the questions of urgency or the questions of immediate interest. That is not to say that such questions are improper, but it is to say that Christian thought can sometimes fall out of balance. One of the realities we face is that in a discussion like this, we are not exactly sure where to begin. Where should we begin talking about beauty?

Allow me to make a couple of preliminary observations, the first of which is this: There is something intrinsic to humanity that is drawn to beauty. There is something of an aesthetic desire in us—an aesthetic appetite. Even infants are attracted to certain objects, and even faces, because of complexity and color and light, those elements that aesthetic theorists have considered the very substance of beauty, form, and attractiveness. Moreover, this desire for and recognition of beauty is something unique to human beings. Dogs do not contemplate a sunset. Animals do not ponder the beauty of the landscape. It is true the heavens are declaring the glory of God, but most of the creatures on the planet are oblivious to this fact. They neither make nor observe nor appreciate art. They stage no dramas, write no music, and paint no portraits. The desire for art is something unique and yet nearly universal among human beings.

At the same time, we must understand that beauty is in crisis; it is a contested category. Let me suggest two reasons why this is so. First, beauty is a category in crisis because it has been so devalued in the reigning confusion of popular culture. The fact is that we have come to use the word *beautiful* in an altogether awkward and inappropriate context. We speak of *beauty,* when what we really mean is *prettiness,* or attractiveness, or even likeability. None of these things, however, is actually equal to beauty. Yet the popular culture increasingly confuses the artificial for the real, the pretty for the beautiful, and the untrue for the true—all of which are essentially based on one root confusion, as we shall see.

Second, beauty is a category in crisis also at the level of elite culture and academia, where philosophers who give attention to aesthetic theory are increasingly convinced that beauty is a shopworn category. It is either political, or entirely subjective, or delusional. Many of the major writers in philosophy suggest that beauty is a category we ought to discard altogether. The idea of beauty, they say, is too expensive, too contested, and too misleading.

In the history of Western thought, beauty has often been a difficult category. The Danish philosopher Søren Kierkegaard, for example, was convinced that in the end aesthetics was a divergence from ethics, so that to be concerned with the beautiful was to be inadequately concerned for the good. Friedrich Nietzche, the very prophet of nihilism himself, believed that the category of beauty was a symptom of the decadence and the weakness of modern humanity. Only the decadent would consider beauty important, he argued, because all that finally matters is power. Perhaps, in reality, Nietzche saw only power as beautiful.

But if beauty is in crisis in terms of the culture, both at the popular level and among the elites, it is also in trouble in the church, where the influence of popular culture has led to confusion about what beauty actually is and why we as Christians should seek it.

A Christian understanding of beauty runs directly into the wisdom of the age by suggesting that the beautiful is simultaneously the good and the true and the real. This goes all the way back to the conversation of the ancients—especially to Plato, who understood the good, the beautiful, the true, and the real as being essentially reducible to the same thing. If there is one good, then that good must also be the true, which must also be the real, which must also be the beautiful. So the good, the beautiful, the true, and the real—the four great historical transcendentals—are unified in the One. For Plato, however, the One had no name.

Augustine, the great theologian of the Patristic Era, identified the One as the one true and living God. Taking Plato's metaphysical speculations into the very heart of the gospel, Augustine suggested that Christians uniquely understand that the good, the beautiful, the true, and the real, are indeed one, because they are established in the reality of the self-revealing God—the triune God of Father, Son, and Holy Spirit. He alone is beautiful, He alone is good, He alone is true, and He alone is real. That is not to suggest that nothing else reflects beauty or truth or goodness. It is simply to say that He alone, by virtue of the fact that He is infinite in all His perfections, is the source and the judge and the end of all that is good, beautiful, true, and real. For as Paul said, "From Him and through Him and to Him are all things. To Him be the glory forever. Amen" (Romans 11:36).

Now, this Christian conversation about the transcendentals opens an entirely new awareness for us. We now begin to understand that there is a moral context and a truth context to every question about beauty. We can no longer talk about beauty as a mere matter of taste. Instantly, by affirming the unity of the transcendentals, we are required to see beauty fundamentally as a matter of truth to which taste is accountable, rather than a matter of taste to which truth is accountable.

Thus, it violates Scripture, and indeed the character of God, to call something "beautiful" that is not good, or "true" that is not beautiful, or "real" that is not true. Yet if we are honest, we admit to ourselves that in our common cultural conversation, we routinely sever the good from the true, the true from the beautiful, the beautiful from the real, and the real from the good. As Christians, we alone really understand why this is so, and why it is so important.

Augustine understood that beauty was a key Christian category. Indeed, Christians cannot properly think as Christians without understanding the power of beauty. In his *Confessions* he said this:

> I have learnt to love you late, Beauty at once so
> ancient and so new! I have learnt to love you late!
> You were within me, and I was in the world out-
> side myself. I searched for you outside myself and,
> disfigured as I was, I fell upon the lovely things of
> your creation. The beautiful things of this world
> kept me from you and yet, if they had not been
> in you, they would have had no being at all.[1]

In that confessional statement, Augustine is saying that it was beauty that was calling him. It was his Creator that was calling him, and yet he was distracted by the things of *apparent* beauty in the world. And yet he does not despise those things; he remembers that their beauty is merely a reflected beauty, derived from the fact that God is their Creator.

Augustine continues:

> It was you then, O Lord, who made them. You
> who are beautiful, for they too are beautiful. You
> who are good, for they too are good. You who
> are, for they too are. But they are not beautiful

---

1. Augustine, *Confessions,* trans. R. S. Pine-Coffin (New York: Penguin, 1961), 231.

and good as you are beautiful and good. Nor do
they have their being as you the Creator have
your being. In comparison with you, they have
neither beauty nor goodness nor being at all.[2]

Augustine realized that in order to see true beauty, he
had to go to his Creator, and then, knowing the Creator,
he might observe the creation and see that it does indeed
bear the mark of its Maker. There is undeniable beauty in
creation, but in comparison with the infinite beauty of
the Creator, such finite beauty no longer has the seductive allure it once had. All earthly beauty is simultaneously validated and relativized by the contemplation of the
beauty of God.

The same theme was picked up by Jonathan Edwards,
who said this:

From what has been said, it is evident, that true
virtue must chiefly consist in love to God; the
Being of beings, infinitely the greatest and best....
For as God is infinitely the greatest Being, so he
is allowed to be infinitely the most beautiful
and excellent: and all the beauty to be found

---

2. Augustine, *Confessions,* 232.

throughout the whole creation, is but the reflection of the diffused beams of that Being who hath an infinite fullness of brightness and glory. God's beauty is infinitely more valuable than that of all other beings.

Edwards continues:

It will also follow from the foregoing things, that God's goodness and love to created beings is derived from, and subordinate to his love to himself.… A truly virtuous mind, being as it were under the sovereign dominion of love to God, above all things, seeks the glory of God, and makes this his supreme, governing, and ultimate end.[3]

In that brief statement, Edwards does something very helpful and very consistent with the Christian tradition. As a matter of fact, it is a necessary insight once we go to the Scriptures. If you search through the Old Testament, you will notice that the word *beauty* is really not there. Instead, you will find the word *glory.* Throughout the

---

3. Jonathan Edwards, *The Nature of True Virtue* (Ann Arbor: The University of Michigan Press, 1960), 14–15, 23, 25.

Bible, the beauty of God is most commonly described as His *glory*. Once we understand the biblical category of glory—that is, the reality of God in terms of His inner reality and the external manifestation of Himself—we realize that God's glory encompasses all the transcendentals. To gaze upon God is not first of all to see His beauty, but rather His *glory.*

Edwards defined *beauty* as consisting mostly in "sweet mutual consents." By this, Edwards meant that things are rightly set: The thing is what God declared that it must be. In other words, beauty is achieved when the thing created most closely and most perfectly glorifies its Creator. Thus a "sweet mutual consent," or absolute harmony, exists between the created thing and the Creator.[4]

When we look at the unity of the transcendentals, and compare Edwards's and Augustine's vision to our contemporary poverty concerning things beautiful, we are quickly and painfully aware that something has gone horribly wrong. Why would human beings seek to sunder the unity between the good and the beautiful, between the true and the real, between the beautiful and the

---

4. The beauty of the world consists wholly of sweet mutual consents, either within itself or with the supreme being. "The Beauty of the World" (c.1725), from the notebook *The Images of Divine Things, The Shadows of Divine Things, The Language and Lessons of Nature* (published 1948).

true? Why would we want to call something that is ugly true? Why would we want to call something that is unreal beautiful? That is a symptom of a human sickness, and that sickness is sin.

Our understanding of beauty as a category in crisis begins not with contemporary confusion, but in the Garden of Eden, where our first parents were attracted to the forbidden fruit at least in part because it was attractive to the eyes. A false understanding of beauty—the false allure of the evil rather than the good—is a part of the story of the Fall. Thus the confusion over beauty is not merely an item of cultural consternation, nor is it merely a matter of theological debate. It is a matter of redemption. The only way out of our confusion over beauty is to know the Creator, to know Him not merely conceptually but personally, and to have our relationship with Him once again set right, something only He can do. Then Edwards's vision of the "sweet mutual consents" might be realized—a redeemed people once again entering into the mutual consent of the good, the beautiful, the true, and the real.

8

A CHRISTIAN VISION OF BEAUTY, PART 2

The Christian vision of beauty opens an entirely new awareness for us. We now begin to understand that there is a moral context, a truth context, to every question about beauty. We can no longer talk about beauty as a mere matter of taste. Instantly, by affirming the unity of the transcendentals, we are required to see beauty fundamentally as a matter of truth to which taste is accountable, rather than a matter of taste to which truth is accountable.

Let me follow through with three basic implications of the Christian vision of truth and beauty. First, the Christian vision of beauty explains why the world is beautiful, but not quite. We are often struck by the beauty of the created order, and this feeling is validated for us in Genesis 1, where the Creator's own verdict is that the creation is good. The goodness of creation is therefore nonnegotiable, and again the unity of the transcendentals reminds us that if it is good, then it is also necessarily true, and real, and beautiful. Thus our metaphysic and our aesthetic, our understanding of truth and our evaluation of ethics, all come together in creation. The creation as God made it was good and beautiful and true and real.

But of course, we then must proceed to Genesis 3, where we learn that the disruption and confusion over beauty—the corruption of the very concept of beauty—is not derived from a mere fault in human perception; it is rather a matter of human rebellion. Genesis 3 is a picture of the beautiful denied, of the real, the good, and the true rejected in favor of mankind's desire to be as God.

The cosmic effect of Adam's fall extended even to the natural world, so that what once could tell only the truth now lies. In verses 6 and 7, we read:

> When the woman saw that the tree was good for
> food, and that it was a delight to the eyes, and
> that the tree was desirable to make one wise, she
> took from its fruit and ate; and she gave also to
> her husband with her, and he ate. Then the eyes
> of both of them were opened, and they knew that
> they were naked; and they sewed fig leaves
> together and made themselves loin coverings.

Thus we are warned that that which is a delight to the eyes may very well be unbeautiful. Our human temptation is to substitute the truly beautiful for that which is merely a delight to our senses or our eyes, and thus we also are drawn to the forbidden fruit of a corrupt and fallen culture.

Verse 7 teaches that once Adam and Eve ate from the Tree of the Knowledge of Good and Evil, their eyes were opened. Following the mentality of the Enlightenment, this would appear not to be a fall at all, but a rise. After all, a human capacity that had been absent is now present. Eyes that have been able to see only the beautiful have been opened, but that opening leads not to enlightenment, but to confusion and corruption. Their eyes were opened, and the first thing they saw was that they were naked. That which had only been seen as beautiful and good and true now became a thing of embarrassment and shame. So Adam and Eve sewed fig leaves together and made themselves loin coverings.

The Creator's verdict upon sin is made clear in the remainder of Genesis 3, and we see again that there are cosmic consequences. The ground itself will demonstrate the effects of the fall. In verses 22–24, we find:

Then the LORD God said, "Behold, the man has become like one of Us, knowing good and evil;

and now, he might stretch out his hand, and take also from the tree of life, and eat, and live forever"—therefore the LORD God sent him out from the garden of Eden, to cultivate the ground from which he was taken. So He drove the man out; and at the east of the garden of Eden He stationed the cherubim and the flaming sword which turned every direction to guard the way to the tree of life.

Because of sin, the earth would now become hostile. That which had willingly yielded its fruit must now be cultivated. By the sweat of the brow, the man would have to work the field, even as the pains of childbirth would also now demonstrate the effect of the fall in the woman herself.

So in Genesis 1, we see the perfection of God's created order—the unity of the transcendentals. Now, however, the unity of the good, the beautiful, the true, and the real has been sundered, and thus we are plunged into confusion and rebellion. Yet even still, the world is beautiful—though not quite. In other words, there is a vestigial beauty in creation that calls out to all concerning the reality of God. This is reflected, of course, throughout the Psalms, where we are reminded that the heavens tell the glories of God. The firmament, the seas, the crawling and creeping things—all of them cry forth the wonder, the reality, and the goodness of the Creator.

Despite this, however, human beings are given to corrupting even this expression of beauty. For one thing, it is all too easy to worship the creation rather than the Creator. We can very quickly look at the creation and think that it is beautiful in itself, rather than having been made beautiful by the One who alone is beautiful. We can begin to look at the human creature as beautiful in and of himself, rather than beautiful because he or she is made in the image of God. Thus we adopt and bring into the very center of our hearts a corrupted understanding of beauty that bears more signs of the fall than of the common grace that allows us—even as fallen creatures—to see this beauty.

There is another problem, of course, with the beauty of creation: It often lies. In the oceans there is a fish known as the lionfish. It is incredibly beautiful—and venomous. In the Amazon jungles there are many frogs, some a beautiful verdant green, some almost unimaginably purple, some almost iridescently yellow—and all deadly, such that the aboriginal peoples in those places would often use the fluid on the skin of these animals to poison their darts. That which looks beautiful to the eyes can kill, and thus we have learned not to trust our apprehension of beauty.

All this confusion about the created world is a symptom of our fallenness, but it is not just human beings that are affected by sin, by the severing of the good, the beautiful, the true, and the real. Creation as a whole finds itself groaning because of human sin. In Romans 8, the apostle Paul speaks of God's work of redemption in all of its comprehensive glory, including creation itself. He writes:

> For the anxious longing of the creation waits
> eagerly for the revealing of the sons of God. For
> the creation was subjected to futility, not willingly,
> but because of Him who subjected it, in hope that
> the creation itself also will be set free from its slavery to corruption into the freedom of the glory of
> the children of God. For we know that the whole
> creation groans and suffers the pains of childbirth
> together until now. And not only this, but also we
> ourselves, having the first fruits of the Spirit, even
> we ourselves groan within ourselves, waiting
> eagerly for our adoption as sons, the redemption
> of our body. (8:19–23)

The work of redemption has cosmic significance. That which has been corrupted by sin is to be restored, but even now in this age we are to see it and understand it as groaning, anxiously awaiting the revelation of the sons of God.

In Revelation 21 we have the end of the story, and even as we began with a perfect creation, we have here the promise of a new heaven and a new earth:

> Then I saw a new heaven and a new earth; for the first heaven and the first earth passed away, and there is no longer any sea. And I saw the holy city, new Jerusalem, coming down out of heaven from God, made ready as a bride adorned for her husband. And I heard a loud voice from the throne, saying, "Behold, the tabernacle of God is among men, and He will dwell among them, and they shall be His people, and God Himself will be among them, and He will wipe away every tear from their eyes; and there will no longer be any death; there will no longer be any mourning, or crying, or pain; the first things have passed away."
>
> And He who sits on the throne said, "Behold, I am making all things new." And He said, "Write, for these words are faithful and true." Then He said to me, "It is done. I am the Alpha and the Omega, the beginning and the end. I will give to the one who thirsts from the

spring of the water of life without cost. He who overcomes will inherit these things, and I will be his God and he will be My son." (verses 1–7)

Beginning in verse 10, John wrote about the new Jerusalem:

And he carried me away in the Spirit to a great and high mountain, and showed me the holy city, Jerusalem, coming down out of heaven from God, having the glory of God. Her brilliance was like a very costly stone, as a stone of crystal-clear jasper. It had a great and high wall, with twelve gates, and at the gates twelve angels; and names were written on them, which are the names of the twelve tribes of the sons of Israel. There were three gates on the east and three gates on the north and three gates on the south and three gates on the west. (verses 10–13)

The beauty of the new Jerusalem is reflected in language about precious and semiprecious stones. The streets are said to be made of gold. All this has been turned into the stuff of gospel music, but the picture is much more of beauty than of opulence. It is meant to cause us to think about what a redeemed city would actually be, how it would appear. This is creation reset, a new heaven and a new earth, and now a new Jerusalem. Thus we have the completion of God's redeeming work, and it comes with the revelation not only of the sons of God, but of the Son of God, the Alpha and the Omega, the Beginning and the End, who after all was the Firstborn of all creation, the One through whom all the worlds were made, and the *Logos* who was the very instrument of the creation itself.

So the Christian worldview explains to us why the world is beautiful—but not quite. As the psalmist wrote, the world indeed tells forth the glory of God, but it does so in fallenness. The world contains things of prettiness that are deadly, and the inclination of human beings is to worship the creature and the creation rather than the Creator. The world is now groaning under the effect of sin and the wrath and judgment of God. That explains a great deal to us, including natural evil—hurricanes and earthquakes and tsunamis, venomous fish and poisonous plants. Yet it was not always so, and it will not always be so. Scripture points us toward the restoration of all things. The Christian understanding of beauty is an eschatological view, one that looks forward to the unveiling of true beauty, which will come on the Day of the Lord when the Alpha and the Omega will be seen as the beautiful One.

9

A CHRISTIAN VISION OF BEAUTY, PART 3

The Christian vision of beauty not only tells us why the world is beautiful—but not quite. Secondly, the Christian worldview explains why the face of a child with Down syndrome is more beautiful than the cover girl in the fashion magazine. The unity of the good, the beautiful, the true, and the real calls us to look below the surface and to understand that the ontological reality of every single human being is that we are made in the image of God. The *imago Dei* is the beauty in each of us, and the rest is but of cosmetic irrelevance.

Just as we, in our fallenness, are likely to see the fallen aspects of creation as beautiful, we are also likely to try to validate ourselves in an artificial humanism of worshiping the creature. When we look at our fellow human beings, or frankly, when we look in the mirror, we are likely to be led astray by prevailing concepts of prettiness and attractiveness rather than to gaze into the mirror or to gaze into our neighbor and see one made in the image of God. The *imago Dei* is the complete and transformative category here, and without it we are left with nothing but the superficial. The *imago Dei* explains why the child with Down syndrome is far more beautiful in herself than the cover girl in the fashion magazine.

First of all, let us remember that one of the transcendentals is the *real*. What does it say of us that we live in a culture in which the cover girl is the ideal, and yet no one actually looks like that? *The Times* of London recently forecast that 80 percent of all women will have cosmetic surgery at some point. What kind of world is this? Now, most of us, and I am the first of sinners in this category, would not want to answer the door to face a television camera first thing in the morning. We get dressed. We use various techniques and technologies. We are at least somewhat attuned to the fashions of the day. So if we suggest that we Christians are completely without concern for attractiveness, we lie. But at the same time, we ought to be the people who understand that this is mere window dressing. This is an apron of fig leaves, placed upon our nakedness in the garden.

In reality, a Christian worldview that takes full account

of human sinfulness is the only way that we can under-stand how prevailing cultural standards tend to dehu-manize our fellow human beings. We delude ourselves into thinking that attractiveness means beauty. Just as nature can lie with its attractive creatures, so also we can lie with the attractiveness we try to portray on the news-stands, on television, in Hollywood, or in the mirror. An entire industry of billions of dollars is built upon the lie that one can buy enough or endure enough, suffer enough or apply enough, to become genuinely beautiful. The whole category of pornography is one big mutual co-conspiracy to deny the beautiful in favor of a perverted ideal of attractiveness. The real is denied, because given the insatiable desire of the sinner toward erotic attractive-ness, the real no longer suffices. Thus the imagined and the fantasized becomes the hunger that is the appetite to be met.

Let me return to the child with Down syndrome. In what way is every single human being beautiful? First of all, it is by virtue of the very fact that every individual is made in the image of God. What if an individual fails to measure up to current cultural or even scientific or med-ical definitions of what it means to be adequately human? We are the people who must say this person is still beau-tiful, still true, still good—not in the sense that we would bless a disease, but in the sense that we would bless the individual who is made in the image of God. Our societal failure to see this is a symptom of something gone terribly wrong in us.

Life is not usually a pretty process. It is not an attractive process. But in its own way, it reflects the beauty of the Creator and His perfect justice, His absolute goodness, and His determination to bring glory to Himself. We should be able to look at the face of a senior saint and see scars and wrinkles and blemishes that have been won through the engagement with the realities of life and say, "You are beautiful!" Remember the good, the beautiful, the true, and the real? We should not wish to hide this. We should not wish to turn away.

I was approached some time ago by a young minister—a new pastor—who made a call upon an elderly lady who was in the hospital. Being like so many young pastors, as all of us who have been in that position can well remember, he was confronted with someone who needed more than he knew how to give. This elderly church member turned to him from her hospital bed and said, "Am I pretty?" He told me, "I lied and said 'Yes.'" The woman was suffering in the last stages of a degenerative disease, and she wasn't pretty. So that pastor's answer was probably the wrong one. I understood his heart, but I told him, "You need to change *pretty* to *beautiful*. This isn't pretty, but it is beautiful." Thus, we can speak of beauty recovered even in that moment when, in a countercultural move, we say pretty really isn't important. In reality, pretty wasn't important when this woman was twelve. Pretty really wasn't important when she was twenty. Pretty is not important now. In heaven, there will be no pretty people, only beautiful saints, made beautiful by the grace of God and for God's glory alone.

The Christian worldview and the Christian vision of beauty explains why the world is beautiful but not quite, and why the face of a child with Down syndrome is more beautiful than the face of the model on the fashion magazine, but thirdly, the Christian understanding of beauty explains why the cross is beautiful and not tragic. Here redemption comes full circle, and our conversation about beauty is directed toward the One who is beautiful and His beautiful cross.

How dare we sing a song like that—about the beauty of the cross? Atheist philosopher Friedrich Nietzche would identify that as one more embrace of weakness by a decadent people who are so delusional that they would give themselves even to embracing the sign of their own vacuous hope. But once again, we are reminded that the beautiful is the good, and the true, and the real. The incarnation is a demonstration of God's beautiful love, and the One who was born in Bethlehem's manger was a beautiful babe. Thus John will say, "We saw His glory, glory as of the only begotten from the Father, full of grace and truth" (John 1:14). Now this glory—this beauty—which is explicitly and wondrously ascribed to the incarnate Lord Jesus Christ, is not attractiveness. It is not prettiness. Indeed the prophet Isaiah said in Isaiah 53:3, "He was despised and forsaken of men, a man of sorrows and acquainted with grief; and like one from whom men hide their face He was despised, and we did not esteem Him."

At the cross, there was no prettiness in Jesus, and the cross itself certainly is not pretty. It is a symbol of execution. Yet we know the reality. We know the truth, and thus we embrace the cross as a beautiful cross on which hung a beautiful Savior, whose death was a beautiful death. In terms of humans, there are no beautiful deaths. Only one death was beautiful, and that was the death of the One who died for our sins.

In 2 Corinthians 4:6, Paul wrote, "For God, who said, 'Light shall shine out of darkness,' is the One who has shone in our hearts to give the Light of the knowledge of the glory of God in the face of Christ." Thus we who have been called to faith, who have come to know the Lord Jesus Christ as Savior and who have been transformed by the grace of God, now see the Lord Jesus Christ and His cross as beautiful.

In Revelation 22, we are reminded of how God will one day bring beauty to perfection:

> Then he showed me a river of the water of life, clear as crystal, coming from the throne of God and of the Lamb, in the middle of its street. On either side of the river was the tree of life, bearing twelve kinds of fruit, yielding its fruit every month; and the leaves of the tree were for the healing of the nations. There will no longer be any curse" [—there's the corruption reversed—] "and the throne of God and of the Lamb will be in it, and His bond-servants will serve Him; they will see His face, and His name will be on their foreheads. And there will no longer be any night; and they will not have need of the light of a lamp nor the light of the sun, because the Lord God will illumine them; and they will reign forever and ever. (verses 1–5)

Let me conclude by suggesting that for Christians, beauty is an evangelistic category. In *The Brothers Karamazov*, Dostoevsky put in the mouth of one of his characters this phrase: "Beauty is the battlefield where God and Satan contend with each other for the hearts of men." And thus it is. In one sense, the Evil One tempts with prettiness, and lies about beauty, and corrupts the good, the beautiful, the true, and the real, sundering them from each other and celebrating the confusion. He celebrates whenever something ugly is called true, when something unreal is called beautiful. Evangelism, then, is a matter of restoring the unity of the transcendentals. The unity that has been sundered, however, can only be put back together again by the One who created the world, and thus redeems.

It is no accident when we are told in Romans 10 that the one who carries the gospel has beautiful feet. A recovery of beauty can only come by recovering humanity. It can only come by recovering truth, and it can only come by recovering the good and the real, by the power of God.

Beauty is for us an evangelistic mandate, a missiological purpose. We are the people who know what beauty is—not that we have seen it yet with our eyes, but we have seen it in a foretaste, and we have been promised it with an assured promise. In this life, we live amidst the pretty, the corrupt, and the artificial. We live among those who do not believe beauty exists, and among those who think beauty can be manufactured. In such a context, we are the ones who have to say we know beauty, and it is none other than Jesus Christ the Lord.

WHAT SHOULD WE THINK OF THE EMERGING CHURCH? PART 1

The "Emerging Church" has become a focus of intense evangelical interest, as the nascent movement has grown in both size and influence. While its eventual shape is not yet clear, we now know enough to draw some preliminary conclusions about the movement, its leaders, and its influence.

In his book *Becoming Conversant with the Emerging Church,* D. A. Carson offers a penetrating analysis of this new movement and its implication. An accomplished scholar with a keen eye on the culture, Carson combines academic scrutiny with a sympathetic understanding of the motivations and cultural experiences that have shaped this new movement.[1]

Carson, research professor of New Testament at Trinity Evangelical Divinity School, demonstrates a bracing understanding of our times and the cultural challenges faced by conservative Christianity. In his 1996 book, *The Gagging of God: Christianity Confronts Pluralism,* he offered an incisive analysis of postmodernism.[2] In that work, Carson's primary focus was epistemology and the postmodern understanding of truth and its knowability. In this new book, Carson continues to focus on truth and knowledge, challenging the Emerging Church at the foundational level of Christian identity.

Carson begins by acknowledging the diversity of the Emerging Church Movement. Given the "porous borders" of the movement, Carson admits that he did not find it "easy to portray it fairly." Nevertheless, after a period of embryonic development, the Emerging Church Movement is now sufficiently mature to offer an understandable model of church and theology, complete with

---

1. D. A. Carson, *Becoming Conversant with the Emerging Church: Understanding a Movement and Its Implications* (Grand Rapids, MI: Zondervan, 2005). All quotes from this book used with permission of Zondervan.

2. D. A. Carson, *The Gagging of God: Christianity Confronts Pluralism* (Grand Rapids, MI: Zondervan, 1996).

understandings of the Bible, the culture, and the Christian message.

The idea of an Emerging Church—whether understood as a movement or a "conversation"—is based in "the conviction that changes in the culture signal that a new church is 'emerging,'" Carson explains. The logic that unites Emerging Church leaders suggests that Christians must respond to the Emerging Church with acceptance and adaptation. "Those who fail to do so are blind to the cultural accretions that hide the gospel behind forms of thought and modes of expression that no longer communicate with the new generation, the emerging generation," Carson relates.

Even though the Emerging Church constitutes an amorphous movement with ill-defined boundaries, Carson is convinced that the influence of the movement is larger than its numbers would suggest.

From what did the Emerging Church emerge? The modern evangelical movement emerged in the last half of the twentieth century, complete with "megachurches" and baby-boomer variations. The Emerging Church is defined over against the massive megachurch models and the seeker-sensitive approaches popular among baby-boomer pastors. The formative leaders of the Emerging Church Movement argue that they are trying to recover a primitive sense of Christian community that, while keenly aware of contemporary culture and deeply engaged with the culture, avoids the consumerism, entertainment-centeredness, and superficiality of mainstream evangelical churches.

It is significant to note that the vast majority of leaders in the Emerging Church Movement seem to have shifted from more conservative forms of evangelical Christianity to the new, more broadly defined Emerging Movement. Carson suggests that a detectable sense of protest fuels the movement. Several of the movement's leaders document their own rejection of older forms of evangelical theology and church life. Some have rejected a dispensational eschatology, while others contrast their new understanding of the culture with a previous experience rooted in fundamentalist separationism.

Carson cites the late Mike Yaconelli, who rejected more conservative forms of evangelical Christianity with a sense of intellectual and cultural condescension. Looking back at his earlier faith, Yaconelli commented: "I realized the modern-institutional-denominational church was permeated by values that are contradictory to the Church of Scripture. The very secular humanism the institutional church criticized pervaded the church structure, language, methodology, process, priorities, values, and vision. The 'legitimate' church, the one that had convinced me of my illegitimacy, was becoming the illegitimate church, fully embracing the values of modernity."[3]

Philosophically, the Emerging Church Movement represents a repudiation of what it identifies as "modernism." While postmodernism is itself a contested category, the leaders of the Emerging Church Movement clearly understand themselves to be affected by, if not fully embracing postmodernism.

In particular, Emerging Church leaders focus on epistemology, arguing that modernism corrupted the church by limiting its focus to a defense of propositional truth based on an unassailable philosophical foundation. The rejection of foundationalism is a central theme of emergent culture.

As Carson explains, a majority of Emerging Church leaders and thinkers hold

> that the fundamental issue in the move from modernism to postmodernism is *epistemology*— i.e., how we know things, or think we know things. Modernism is often pictured as pursuing truth, absolutism, linear thinking, rationalism,

---

3. Carson, *Becoming Conversant with the Emerging Church*, 20.

certainty, the cerebral as opposed to the affec-
tive—which in turn breeds arrogance, inflexibility,
a lust to be right, the desire to control. Postmodernism, by contrast, recognizes how much of what
we "know" is shaped by the culture in which we
live, is controlled by emotions and aesthetics and
heritage, and in fact can only be intelligently held
as part of a common tradition, without overbear-
ing claims to being true or right.[4]

At this point, Carson focuses on Brian McLaren,
probably the most articulate speaker in the Emerging
Movement. McLaren has written a small library of
works promoting and defining the Emerging Church
Movement. Though the movement has many formative
leaders, McLaren is undoubtedly the most influential
thinker among them. To a large and undeniable extent,
McLaren has succeeded in branding the Emerging
Church Movement.

The very nomenclature of the movement betrays a
sense that evangelicalism must be cast aside in order for
something new, radical, and more authentic to emerge.
"For almost everyone within the movement," Carson

---

4. Carson, *Becoming Conversant with the Emerging Church*, 27.

argues, "this works out in an emphasis on feelings and affections over against linear thought and rationality; on experience over against truth; on inclusion over against exclusion; on participation over against individualism and the heroic loner."[5] This approach produces what McLaren calls "a new kind of Christian," and a new kind of church.[6]

Accepting the postmodern insistence that "metanarratives" are dead, McLaren argues that Christianity must develop a new way of describing, defining, and defending the gospel. A metanarrative—a unifying theory of universal meaning—is to be replaced by a far more humble understanding of truth that accepts pluralism as a given and holds all truth-claims under suspicion.

Postmodernism insists that truth-claims must be presented in a humbled form, without claims of universal validity, objectivity, or absoluteness.

Carson criticizes the majority of Emerging Church leaders as relying on a facile and simple antithesis— "namely, modernism is bad and postmodernism is good." He credits Brian McLaren with a more sophisticated understanding of postmodernism's dangers. Nevertheless,

---

5. Carson, *Becoming Conversant with the Emerging Church,* 29.
6. Brian D. McLaren, *A New Kind of Christian: A Tale of Two Friends on a Spiritual Journey* (San Francisco: Jossey-Bass, 2001).

he also criticizes McLaren for holding that "absolutism is associated with modernism, so that every evaluation he offers on that side of the challenge is negative." McLaren may dismiss religious relativism, but Carson argues that he does not critique it. As Carson reflects, "I have not seen from McLaren, or anyone else in the emerging church movement, a critique of any substantive element of postmodern thought."[7]

In his opening chapter, Carson focuses on a workshop led by Brian McLaren at a conference for Emerging Church leaders. When asked about the issue of homosexuality, McLaren insisted that there is no good and satisfactory position for Christians to take, because all positions will hurt someone, and, as Carson explains McLaren's position, "that is always bad." McLaren also took refuge in the assumption that homosexuality as we know it today may not be the behavior or phenomenon so roundly condemned in the Bible.

In focusing on this workshop, Carson's concern is not primarily the issue of homosexuality itself. Instead, he understands that McLaren's carefully nuanced non-answer to the question is illustrative of the Emerging Church Movement's failure to render clear answers in the aftermath of a rejection of absolute truth.

7. Carson, *Becoming Conversant with the Emerging Church,* 36.

In a perceptive footnote, Carson makes an interesting comparison: "It is impossible to find in the writings of, say, Brian McLaren, an utterance akin to that of Luther at the Diet of Worms." Instead, many in the Emerging Church Movement prefer to take refuge in an either/or, both/and, and inherently ambiguous understanding of truth. All this leads Carson to ask a crucial question: "Is there at least some danger that what is being advocated is not so much a new kind of Christian in a new emerging church, but a church that is so submerging itself in the culture that it risks hopeless compromise?"[8] In the end, that question can be answered only by a careful look at what Emerging Church leaders actually believe and teach. They have certainly given us plenty of material to consider.

---

8. Carson, *Becoming Conversant with the Emerging Church,* 43–44.

WHAT SHOULD WE THINK OF THE EMERGING CHURCH? PART 2

The Emerging Church Movement includes an expanding number of leaders and a diversity of representations. For some, the movement appears to be something of a generational phenomenon—a way for younger evangelicals to reshape evangelical identity and relate to their own culture. For others, the connection with the Emerging Church Movement seems to be a matter of mood rather than methodology or theory. Elements of worship, aesthetics, and cultural iconography common to the Emerging Church Movement have been embraced by a cohort of younger evangelicals, who nonetheless hold to the indispensability of propositional truth. Nevertheless, for most Emerging Church leaders, the movement appears to be an avenue for reshaping Christianity in a new mold.

The philosophical maneuvers borrowed from postmodern theory provide a mechanism for transcending the defensive posture against Enlightenment criticism that mainstream Christianity has had to assume for most of the last three hundred years. By denying that truth is propositional, Emerging Church theorists avoid and renounce any responsibility to defend many of the doctrines long considered essential to the Christian faith.

In *Becoming Conversant with the Emerging Church,* D. A. Carson attempts to measure the Emerging Church Movement on its own terms—and then offers a critical analysis of the movement from a larger perspective.

When Emerging Church leaders point to a massive cultural shift in Western societies, they are not seeing an illusion. As Carson acknowledges, "The emerging church movement honestly tries to read the culture in which we find ourselves and to think through the implications of such a reading for our witness, our grasp of theology, our churchmanship, even our self-understanding."[1] Something remarkable has occurred in the culture, and Emerg-

---

1. D. A. Carson, *Becoming Conversant with the Emerging Church: Understanding a Movement and Its Implications* (Grand Rapids, MI: Zondervan, 2005), 45.

ing Church leaders certainly have a point in criticizing mainstream evangelicalism for missing this crucial fact.

Emerging Church leaders focus most of their negative criticism on what they identify as modernist thinking. The mainstream evangelical movement is criticized for having succumbed to the temptation to accept modernity's limitation of truth to propositions, and therefore also the responsibility to defend those propositions against Enlightenment-based attacks. Emerging Church theorists dismiss what they identify as "foundationalist" thinking among conservative evangelicals, and feel themselves to be liberated from foundationalist assumptions insofar as they redefine truth in terms of narrative, communal understanding, and epistemological humility.

Yet, as Carson accurately levels his criticism, Emerging Church leaders demonstrate an incredible naiveté about the nature of postmodernism. As Carson summarizes, "The postmodern ethos tends to be anti-absolutist, suspicious of truth claims, and wide open to relativism. It tends to adopt therapeutic approaches to spirituality, and—whether despite the individualism of the Western heritage or perhaps even because of it—it is often attracted to communitarian wholeness."[2]

---

2. Carson, *Becoming Conversant with the Emerging Church,* 48.

Emerging Church leaders, influenced by postmodern theory, rightly understand that every individual is deeply embedded in a social location. They are certainly correct in accusing much of mainstream evangelicalism from missing this point entirely—blissfully unaware of how the ambient culture has influenced our own ways of thinking. But does an acknowledgment of the role of social location relativize the meaning of a text?

Carson, a capable and insightful critic of postmodernism, acknowledges that the postmodern approach has been effective in exposing the weaknesses of some forms of modernism. Furthermore, Carson also credits postmodernism with encouraging us to be "open to thinking about nonlinear and methodologically unrigorous factors in human knowing."[3] In addition, even as the modern age was characterized by embarrassing claims of cultural superiority, postmodernism has insisted on sensitivity to the diversity of cultures found in the global context.

Carson also credits postmodernism with the affirmation that human knowledge is always marked by finitude. "We get things wrong not only because we are not omniscient," Carson admits, "but also because we are corrupt, morally blind, painfully selfish, and given to excuses and self-justification."[4]

---

3. Carson, *Becoming Conversant with the Emerging Church*, 103.
4. Carson, *Becoming Conversant with the Emerging Church*, 104.

Where does all this lead us? As Carson understands, a necessary and appropriate critique of evangelical habits of thinking—including unhealthy influences from modernist thinking—should be welcomed by serious-minded evangelicals. Yet:

> Once we have acknowledged the unavoidable finiteness of all human knowers, the cultural diversity of the human race, the diversity of factors that go into human knowing, and even the evil that lurks in the human breast and easily perverts claims of knowledge into totalitarian control and lust for power—once we have acknowledged these things, is there any way left for us to talk about knowing what is true or objectively real? Hard postmodernists insist there is not. And that's the problem.[5]

At this point, Carson levels his guns at the most extreme and irresponsible forms of postmodern thinking. He accuses postmodern theorists of channeling the discussion into "a manipulative antithesis" between an arrogant claim to possess full and omniscient knowledge and a radical and dishonest humility that claims that truth is fundamentally unknowable.

---

5. Carson, *Becoming Conversant with the Emerging Church*, 104.

Beyond this, the "hard" postmodernists also fail to acknowledge that, even though language is complex and communication is uneven, some degree of communication does take place. A deep inconsistency in postmodern thinking is apparent when radical postmodernists write books, give speeches, or engage in conversation. If the communication of truth is as ambiguous, awkward, and uneven as the postmodernists argue, why write books?

While all thinkers fall prey to the trap of inconsistency, the postmodernists seem to embrace inconsistency as an intellectual virtue. As Carson suggests, even as they suggest that all scientific knowledge is produced by a process of social construction, "apparently they exclude their own knowledge of this analysis from a similar charge."[6]

In the end, Carson's presentation and criticism of postmodernism sets the stage for his most focused analysis of the Emerging Church. He acknowledges that many, if not all, of the Emerging Church leaders appear to be driven by a genuine desire to reach persons either unreached or alienated from what they have understood to be the Christian gospel. Nevertheless, Carson appears convinced that the Emerging Church Movement, as represented by its most influential founders and leaders, has

---

6. Carson, *Becoming Conversant with the Emerging Church*, 9.

embraced an understanding of Christianity that is inherently unstable, often sub-biblical, and dangerously evasive when it comes to matters of truth.

Carson's book makes for mandatory reading—at least for all those who are concerned about the Emerging Church and the future of evangelical Christianity. He combines a charity of spirit with clarity of thought. If anything, Carson demonstrates an honest attempt to understand the Emerging Church Movement on its own terms. Yet, in the final analysis, Carson sounds an alarm.

After discussing at length the philosophical and cultural background to the Emerging Church Movement and after tracing the epistemological implications of the movement's embrace of postmodern theory, Carson turns to doctrine.

At this point, Carson's critique grows sharper and clearer. He considers the writings of Brian McLaren and Steve Chalke as representative of the movement and its doctrinal dangers. Carson's most important and incisive criticism is focused on the question of Christ's atonement and its meaning.

Given the fact that both McLaren and Chalke deny the substitutionary nature of the atonement—indeed, rejecting virtually any notion of penal substitution—Carson sees the ghost of a discredited theological liberalism.

"I have to say, as kindly but as forcefully as I can, that to my mind, if words mean anything, both McLaren and Chalke have largely abandoned the gospel," Carson laments.

> Perhaps their rhetoric and enthusiasm have led them astray and they will prove willing to reconsider their published judgments on these matters and embrace biblical truth more holistically than they have been doing in their most recent works. But if not, I cannot see how their own words constitute anything less than a drift toward abandoning the gospel itself.[7]

Where are the other leaders of the Emerging Church on this question? I am constantly confronted by young pastors who identify themselves with the Emerging Church Movement but deny that they associate themselves with the aberrant theological impulses and outright doctrinal denials that characterize the writings of the movement's most well-known and influential leaders.

I completely agree with D. A. Carson when he reflects: "I would feel much less worried about the direc-

---

7. Carson, *Becoming Conversant with the Emerging Church,* 186–187.

tions being taken by other emerging church leaders if these leaders would rise up and call McLaren and Chalke to account where they have clearly abandoned what the Bible actually says."[8]

There is a thin-skinned sensitivity on the part of many of those who identify with the Emerging Church. Even as they level severe and unstinting criticism at the inherited evangelical models, they recoil from criticism directed at their own proposals. The issues at stake in this controversy transcend sensitivities and are far too important to be sidelined in the name of uncritical acceptance. As always, truth remains the ultimate issue.

Carson puts this especially well:

The gospel is deeply and unavoidably tied to truths, truths of various sorts. Our ability to know such truths (never exhaustively) and obey them turns on many factors: direct revelation from God (not least in matters concerning the nature and character of God), the illumination of the Spirit, and, for the ineluctable historical elements of the gospel, on historical witnesses and the records they have left. And we increase such biblical faith

---

8. Carson, *Becoming Conversant with the Emerging Church*, 187.

by being crystal clear on the convincing nature of the evidence so graciously provided. Alternatively, the same presentation may simply repel some who hear us, precisely because it is truth itself that guarantees unbelief in the hearts and minds of some.[9]

Contemporary evangelicals face the responsibility, not only of becoming conversant with the Emerging Church, but of continuing a conversation about what this movement really represents and where its trajectory is likely to lead. Some of the best, brightest, and most sensitive and insightful individuals from the younger evangelical generation have been drawn to this movement. Undoubtedly, they have much to offer in terms of legitimate criticism of mainstream evangelicalism. The evangelical movement is far too immersed in pragmatism, experientialism, consumerism, and anti-intellectualism. Evangelicals seem only too eager to provide evidence of cultural isolationism and an eccentric grasp of cultural priorities.

Beyond all this, far too many evangelicals seem unconcerned about the absence of authentic ecclesiology—failing to see a vision of the church that is driven by the

---

9. Carson, *Becoming Conversant with the Emerging Church,* 216.

very missional and incarnational priorities that drive many within the Emerging Church Movement.

The real question is this: Will the future leaders of the Emerging Church acknowledge that, while truth is always more than propositional, it is never less? Will they come to affirm that a core of nonnegotiable doctrines constitutes a necessary set of boundaries to authentic Christian faith? Will they embrace an understanding of Christianity that reforms the evangelical movement without denying its virtues?

At the same time, the tables must be turned. Will evangelicals be willing to direct hard and honest critical analysis at our own cultural embeddedness, intellectual faults, and organizational hubris?

The Emerging Church and its leaders are right to insist that substance must be preferred to superficiality. We can only pray and hope that they will remember and acknowledge that substance requires a substantial and honest embrace of truth.

_____ **12**

A GENEROUS ORTHODOXY

Is It Orthodox?

In the last two chapters, I mentioned a prominent figure in the Emergent Church Movement, Brian D.
McLaren. His recent book's title looks both promising
and inspiring. *A Generous Orthodoxy* is sure to get attention, and its title grabs both heart and mind.[1] Who
wouldn't want to embrace an orthodoxy of generosity?
On the other hand, the title raises an unavoidable question: Just how "generous" can orthodoxy be?

---

1. Brian McLaren, *A Generous Orthodoxy* (Grand Rapids, MI: Zondervan,
   2004).

McLaren is the founding pastor of Cedar Ridge Community Church near Baltimore, and he has become a leading figure—if not the single most influential figure—in what is now known as the Emergent Church. In *A Generous Orthodoxy,* he offers what amounts to a manifesto for the Emergent Church Movement, even as he claims to have established a position that combines the strengths of both liberalism and evangelicalism, the charismatic and the contemplative, the mystical and the poetic.

McLaren defines *orthodoxy* as "straight thinking" or "right opinion." He sets the mood of his book right at the start: "The last thing I want is to get into nauseating arguments about why this or that form of theology (dispensational, covenant, charismatic, whatever) or methodology (cell church, megachurch, liturgical church, seeker church, blah, blah, blah) is right (meaning approaching or achieving timeless technical perfection)." Still following?

Since he is determined to transcend all those difficult questions of who is right and who is wrong, McLaren wants to qualify his brand of orthodoxy as "generous orthodoxy." He credits the term to Dr. Stanley Grenz, a prominent revisionist evangelical theologian who, in his book *Renewing the Center,* quotes the late Yale theologian Hans Frei as the inventor of the phrase.[2]

---

2. McLaren, *A Generous Orthodoxy,* 28.

McLaren intends to be provocative, explaining that this reflects his "belief that clarity is sometimes overrated, and that shock, obscurity, playfulness, and intrigue (carefully articulated) often stimulate more thought than clarity."[3]

McLaren is also honest about the fact that he lacks any formal theological education. As a matter of fact, he seems rather proud of this fact, insinuating that formal theological education is likely to trap persons in a habit of trying to determine right belief.

This author's purpose is transparent and consistent. Following the worldview of the postmodern age, he embraces relativism at the cost of clarity in matters of truth and intends to redefine Christianity for this new age, largely in terms of an eccentric mixture of elements he would take from virtually every theological position and variant.

He claims to uphold "consistently, unequivocally, and unapologetically" the historic creeds of the church, specifically the Apostles' and Nicene Creeds.[4] At the same time, however, he denies that truth should be articulated in propositional form, and thus undercuts his own "unequivocal" affirmation. McLaren doesn't like answering

---

3. McLaren, *A Generous Orthodoxy,* 27.
4. McLaren, *A Generous Orthodoxy,* 32.

questions, either. Even though he would be more appropriately categorized as a "post-evangelical," McLaren was listed as one of twenty-five influential evangelicals in the February 7, 2005, edition of *Time* magazine. In its profile, *Time* referred to a conference at which McLaren was addressed with a question related to gay marriage. "You know what," McLaren responded, "the thing that breaks my heart is that there's no way I can answer it without hurting someone on either side."[5] *Time* referred to this as "a kinder and gentler brand of religion." Others would be less charitable, for McLaren's "non-answer" is itself an answer. This is a man who doesn't want to offend anyone on any side of any argument. That's why it's hard to find the orthodoxy in *A Generous Orthodoxy*.

As McLaren admits, "People who try to label me an exclusivist, inclusivist, or universalist on the issue of hell will find here only more reason for frustration."[6] In other words, McLaren simply refuses to answer the question as to whether there will be anyone in hell. He refers to these questions—evangelical hang-ups for the doctrinally moribund—as "weapons of mass distraction."

McLaren effectively ransacks the Christian tradition,

---

5. "The Twenty-five Most Influential Evangelicals in America," *Time,* February 7, 2005.

6. McLaren, *A Generous Orthodoxy,* 42.

picking and choosing among theological options without any particular concern for consistency. He rejects the traditional understanding of doctrine as statements of biblical truth and instead presents a variant of postmodernism—effectively arguing that doctrines form a language that is meaningful to Christians, even if not objectively true. He claims to be arguing for "a generous third way beyond the conservative and liberal versions of Christianity so dominant in the Western world."[7]

Incredibly, McLaren simply asserts that concern for the propositional truthfulness of the text is an artifact of the modern age, "modern-Western-moderately-educated desires."[8] As a postmodernist, he considers himself free from any concern for propositional truthfulness and simply wants the Christian community to embrace a pluriform understanding of truth as a way out of doctrinal conflict and impasse.

What about other belief systems? McLaren suggests that we should embrace the existence of different faiths, "willingly, not begrudgingly." What would this mean? Well, a complete reconsideration of Christian missions, for one thing. McLaren claims to affirm that Christians

---

7. McLaren, *A Generous Orthodoxy,* 115.
8. McLaren, *A Generous Orthodoxy,* 178.

should give witness to their faith in Jesus Christ. But, before you assume this means an affirmation of Christian missions, consider this statement:

> I must add, though, that I don't believe making disciples must equal making adherents to the Christian religion. It may be advisable in many (not all!) circumstances to help people become followers of Jesus *and* remain within their Buddhist, Hindu, or Jewish contexts. This will be hard, you say, and I agree. But frankly, it's not at all easy to be a follower of Jesus in many "Christian" religious contexts, either.[9]

Citing missiologist David Bosch, McLaren affirms that we have no assurance that salvation is found outside the work of Jesus Christ. Nevertheless, he believes that we cannot jump from this to a claim that there is no salvation outside belief in Jesus Christ.

The Bible, McLaren argues, is intended to equip God's people for good works. He rejects words such as *authority, inerrancy,* and *infallibility* as unnecessary and distracting. In a previous work, McLaren had argued that

---

9. McLaren, *A Generous Orthodoxy,* 293.

the Bible is "a unique collection of literary artifacts that together support the telling of an amazing and essential story."[10] His thinking shows the influence of the so-called Yale School of theologians who have argued for Scripture as the record and substance of Christianity as a "cultural-linguistic system," to be interpreted as narrative and not as propositional truth.

The Emergent Church Movement represents a significant challenge to biblical Christianity. Unwilling to affirm that the Bible contains propositional truths that form the framework for Christian belief, this movement argues that we can have Christian symbolism and substance without those thorny questions of truthfulness that have so vexed the modern mind. The worldview of postmodernism—complete with an epistemology that denies the possibility of or need for propositional truth—affords the movement an opportunity to hop, skip, and jump throughout the Bible and the history of Christian thought in order to take whatever pieces they want from one theology and attach them, like doctrinal Post-it notes, to whatever picture they would want to draw.

When it comes to issues such as the exclusivity of the

---

10. Brian D. McLaren and Tony Campolo, *Adventures in Missing the Point* (Grand Rapids, MI: Zondervan), 75.

gospel, the identity of Jesus Christ as both fully human and fully divine, the authoritative character of Scripture as written revelation, and the clear teachings of Scripture concerning issues such as homosexuality, this movement simply refuses to answer the questions.

McLaren attributes this to humility. "A generous orthodoxy," he explains, "in contrast to the tense, narrow, controlling, or critical orthodoxies of so much of Christian history, doesn't take itself too seriously. It is humble; it doesn't claim too much; it admits it walks with a limp."[11] In other words, it is so humble that it will not answer some questions that will not rest without an answer. In this case, a non-answer is an answer. A responsible theological argument must acknowledge that difficult questions demand to be answered. We are not faced with an endless array of doctrinal variants from which we can pick and choose. Homosexuality either will or will not be embraced as normative. The church either will or will not accept a radical re-visioning of the missionary task. We will either see those who have not come to faith in the Lord Jesus Christ as persons to whom we should extend a clear gospel message and a call for decision, or we will simply come alongside them to tell our story as they tell their own.

---

11. McLaren, *A Generous Orthodoxy,* 155.

The problem with *A Generous Orthodoxy*, as the author must surely recognize, is that this orthodoxy bears virtually no resemblance to orthodoxy as it has been known and affirmed by the church throughout the centuries. Honest Christians know that disagreements over issues of biblical truth are inevitable. But we owe each other at least the honesty of taking a position, arguing for that position from Scripture, and facing the consequences of our theological convictions.

Orthodoxy must be generous, but it cannot be so generous that it ceases to be orthodox. Inevitably, Christianity asserts truths that, to the postmodern mind, will appear decidedly ungenerous. Nevertheless, this is the truth that leads to everlasting life. The gospel simply is not up for renegotiation in the twenty-first century. A true Christian generosity recognizes the infinitely generous nature of the truth that genuinely saves. Accept no substitutes.

13

IT TAKES ONE
TO KNOW ONE

Liberalism as Atheism

"I t takes one to know one," quipped historian Eugene Genovese, then an atheist and Marxist. He was referring to liberal Protestant theologians, whom he believed to be closet atheists. As Genovese observed, "When I read much Protestant theology and religious history today, I have the warm feeling that I am in the company of fellow nonbelievers."[1]

Genovese's comment rang prophetic when Gerd Lüdemann, a prominent German theologian, declared a

---

1. Eugene Genovese, *The Southern Front: History and Politics in the Cultural War* (Columbia, MO: University of Missouri Press, 1995), 9–10.

few years ago, "I no longer describe myself as a Christian." A professor of New Testament and director of the Institute of Early Christian Studies at Gottingen University in Germany, Lüdemann has provoked the faithful and denied essential Christian doctrines for many years.

With amazing directness, Lüdemann has denied the resurrection of Jesus, the virgin birth, and eventually the totality of the gospel. Claiming to practice theology as a "scientific discipline," Lüdemann (who taught for several years at the Vanderbilt Divinity School) has sought to debunk or discredit the Bible as an authoritative source for Christian theology. [2]

In his influential book *Heretics* (1996), Lüdemann sought to demonstrate that the heretics were right all along and that the Christian church had conjured a supernatural Jesus to further its own cause. In *What Really Happened to Jesus* (1995) he argued, "We can no longer take the statements about the resurrection of Jesus literally." Lest anyone miss his point, Lüdemann continued, "So let us say quite specifically: *the tomb of Jesus was not empty, but full, and his body did not disappear, but rotted away.*"[3]

---

2. "Theologian Abandons Christianity," *Christian Century,* June 17–24, 1998, 606.

3. Gerd Lüdemann, *What Really Happened to Jesus,* trans. John Bowden (Louisville, KY: Westminster John Knox Press, 1995), 134–135.

Nevertheless, Lüdemann argued that Christianity could be rescued from its naive supernaturalism by focusing on the moral teachings of Jesus. Later, Lüdemann gave an interview to the German magazine *Evangelische Kommentare* in which he stated that the Bible's portrayal of Jesus is a "fairy-tale world which we cannot enter."[4]

In that same interview he denied the sinlessness of Jesus, explaining that, if Jesus was truly human, "we must grant that he was neither sinless or without error." The church, he argued, must give up its faith in the "risen Lord" and settle for Jesus as a mere human being, but one from whom much can be learned.

In later writings, Lüdemann argued that Jesus was conceived as the product of a rape, and stated clearly that he could no longer "take my stand on the Apostles' Creed" or any other historic confession of faith. He continued, however, to teach as an official member of the theology faculty—a post that requires the certification of the Lutheran Church in Germany.

Gerd Lüdemann's theological search-and-destroy mission eventually ran him down a blind alley. As he told the Swiss Protestant news agency *Reformierter Pressedienst,* he has come to a new realization. "A Christian is someone who prays to Christ and believes in what is

---

4. Also documented in Lüdemann's *The Unholy in Holy Scripture*, xiii.

promised by Christian doctrine. So I asked myself: 'Do I pray to Jesus, do I pray to the God of the Bible?' And I don't do that. Quite the reverse."[5]

Having come face-to-face with his unbelief, Lüdemann has now turned his guns on church bureaucrats and liberal theologians. Many church officials, Lüdemann claims, no longer believe in the creeds, but simply "interpret" the words into meaninglessness. Liberal theologians, he asserts, try to reformulate Christian doctrine into something they can believe, and still claim to be Christians. He now describes liberal theology as "contemptible."

Looking back on the whole project of liberal theology, Professor Lüdemann offered an amazing reflection: "I don't think Christians know what they mean when they proclaim Jesus as Lord of the world. That is a massive claim. If you took that seriously, you would probably have to be a fundamentalist. If you can't be a fundamentalist, then you should give up Christianity for the sake of honesty."[6]

Professor Gerd Lüdemann reveals much about the true state of modern liberal theology. One core doctrine

5. "Theologian Abandons Christianity," *Christian Century*, June 17–24, 1998, 606.

6. "Theologian Abandons Christianity," *Christian Century*.

after another has fallen by liberal denial—all in the name of salvaging the faith in the modern age. The game is now reaching its end stage. Having denied virtually every essential doctrine, the liberals are holding an empty bag. As Lüdemann suggests, they should give up their claim on Christianity for the sake of honesty.

Professor Lüdemann is now a formidable foe of liberal theology, but he is also one of its victims. He said that he plans to pick up his teaching career from a "post-Christian" perspective, now that he knows "what I am and what I am not." Should his liberal colleagues attempt to remove him from the theology faculty as a "post-Christian," Lüdemann may respond with Genovese's quip: "It takes one to know one."

14

THE OPENNESS OF GOD AND THE FUTURE OF EVANGELICAL THEOLOGY

Theology was front and center at the 2003 meeting of the Evangelical Theological Society in Atlanta, Georgia. It was not a year for business as usual, for the society would be confronting charges brought against two of its members. Given the nature of the charges, one or both of these individuals could be removed from membership in the society. Why? The answer to that question points to one of the most significant controversies facing contemporary evangelicals.

The theologians in question, Clark Pinnock and John Sanders, are both proponents of a theological movement known as "Open Theism." In sum, open theists argue for a new model of understanding God's knowledge—a model that insists that true human freedom requires that God cannot know human decisions in advance.

Actually, open theists deny God's omniscience in matters that go beyond human decisions. The worldview promoted by open theists is based in a high degree of confidence that God will be able to direct the future in a general way, but open theists deny that God can possess infallible and comprehensive knowledge of the future. In essence, God is waiting, with the rest of us, to know how any number of issues will turn out.

Promoted by Pinnock and Sanders, along with other popular theologians such as Gregory Boyd, the open theists present a more user-friendly deity, less offensive to many moderns. This new model of God, based in something like what Clark Pinnock calls "creative love theism," redefines the God of the Bible and denies the classical understanding of God's sovereignty, knowledge, and power.

Bruce Ware, a careful critic of open theism, summarizes the movement in this way:

> This movement takes its name from the fact that
> its adherents view much of the future as "open"

rather than closed, even to God. Much of the
future, that is, is yet undecided, and hence it is
unknown to God. God knows all that can be
known, open theists assure us. But future free
choices and actions, because they haven't happened yet, do not exist, and so God (even God)
cannot know them.[1]

As Ware explains, "God cannot know what does not
exist, they claim, and since the future does not now exist,
God cannot know it." Most importantly, open theists
argue that God cannot know what free creatures will
choose or do in the future. Thus, "God learns moment-
by-moment what we do, when we do it, and His plans
must constantly be adjusted to what actually happens, in
so far as this is different than what He anticipated."[2]

In two important books, *God's Lesser Glory: The
Diminished God of Open Theism* and *Their God Is Too
Small: Open Theism and the Undermining of Confidence
in God,* Ware provides a responsible and careful analysis
of the open theists' arguments. Ware takes these thinkers
seriously, and judges their argument by the Bible. In so
doing, he concludes that the open view of God "poses a

---

1. Bruce Ware, *Their God Is Too Small* (Wheaton, IL: Crossway, 2003), 12.
2. Ware, *Their God Is Too Small,* 12–13.

challenge to the evangelical church that is unparalleled in this generation."[3]

The doctrine of God is the central organizing principle of Christian theology, and it establishes the foundation of all other theological principles. Evangelical Christians believe in the unity of truth. Therefore, a shift in the doctrine of God—much less of this consequence—necessarily implies shifts and transformations in all other doctrines.

The open theists point to biblical passages that speak of God repenting or changing His mind. Rather than interpreting those passages in keeping with the explicit statements of Scripture that God knows the future perfectly, the open theists turn the theological system on its head and interpret the clear teaching of Scripture through the narratives—rather than the other way around.

They also counsel that their "open" view of God is more helpful than classical Christian theism. After all, they advise, it allows God "off the hook" when things do not go as we had hoped.

In a now notorious example, Greg Boyd tells of a woman whose plans for missionary service were ruined by the adultery of her husband and subsequent divorce.

---

3. Ware, *Their God Is Too Small*, 129.

This woman, Boyd relates, went to her pastor for counsel, asking him how God could have led her to have married this young man, only to see the marriage end in adultery and disaster. This pastor assured the woman that God shared her surprise and disappointment in how the young man turned out.[4]

Most evangelicals would be shocked to meet this updated model of God face-to-face. Nevertheless, subtle shifts in evangelical conviction have been undermining Christianity's biblical concept of God.

Belief in God's absolute knowledge has united theologians in the evangelical, Catholic, and Orthodox traditions. Denials of divine omniscience have been limited to heretical movements like the Socinians. Even where Calvinists and Arminians have differed on the relationship between the divine will and foreknowledge, they have stood united in affirming God's absolute, comprehensive, and unconditional knowledge of the future.

Several years ago, a major study of religious belief revealed just how radically our culture has compromised the doctrine of God. Sociologists asked the question, "Do you believe in a God who can change the course of events

---

4. Greg Boyd, *God of the Possible* (Grand Rapids, MI: Baker, 2000), 103–106.

on earth?" One answer, which became the title of the study, was "No, just the ordinary one." That is to say, modern men and women seem to feel no need to believe in a God who can change the course of events on earth—just an "ordinary God" who is an innocent bystander observing human events.[5]

Measured against the biblical revelation, this is not God at all. The God of the Bible is not a bystander in human events. Throughout the Scriptures, God speaks of His own unlimited power, sovereign will, and perfect knowledge.

This model of divine sovereignty is explicitly denied by the open theists. As Clark Pinnock explains, "God is sovereign according to the Bible in the sense of having the power to exist in himself and the power to call forth the universe out of nothing by his Word. But God's sovereignty does not have to mean what some theists and atheists claim, namely, the power to determine each detail in the history of the world."[6]

The obvious question to ask at this point is this: Just which details does God choose to determine? Pinnock's

5. Grace Davie, *Religion in Britain since 1945: Believing without Belonging* (Oxford: Blackwell, 1994), 79.

6. Clark Pinnock, et al. *Predestination and Free Will* (Downers Grove, IL: InterVarsity, 1986), 145.

"creative love theism" is, regardless of his intentions, a way of taking theism out of theology. This God is so redefined that He bears little resemblance to the God of the Bible.

Pinnock and his colleagues argue that evangelicals must transform our understanding of God into a model that is more "culturally compelling." Where does this end? The culture gets to define our model of God?

Open theism does not stand alone. Acceptance of this model will require a complete transformation of evangelical conviction. A redefinition of the doctrine of God leads immediately to the redefinition of the gospel. A reformulation of our understanding of God's knowledge leads inescapably to a reformulation of how God relates to the world.

Indeed, some have gone so far as to call for an "evangelical megashift" that would completely transform evangelical conviction for a new generation. Even granting the open theist the highest motivations, the result of their theological transformation would be unmitigated disaster for the church.

The late B. B. Warfield remarked that God could be removed altogether from some systematic theologies without any material impact on the other doctrines in the system. My fear is that this indictment can be generalized of much contemporary evangelical theology. As the culture draws to a close, evangelicals are not arguing over the denominational issues that marked the debate of the twentieth century's early years. The issues are now far more serious.

Sadly, evangelicals are now debating the central doctrine of Christian theism. The question is whether evangelicals will affirm and worship the sovereign and purposeful God of the Bible, or shift their allegiance to the limited God of the modern megashift.

At stake is not only the future of the Evangelical Theological Society, but of evangelical theology itself. Regardless of how the votes went in Atlanta, this issue is likely to remain on the front burner of evangelical attention for years to come.

The debate over open theism is another reminder that theology is too important to be left to the theologians. Open theism must be a matter of concern for the whole church. This much is certain—God will not change based on how a vote turns out.

15

THE DEMISE OF CHURCH DISCIPLINE, PART 1

What is pure is corrupted much more
quickly than what is corrupt is purified.

—JOHN CASSIAN (AD 360–435)

The decline of church discipline is perhaps the most visible failure of the contemporary church. No longer concerned with maintaining purity of confession or lifestyle, the contemporary church sees itself as a voluntary association of autonomous members, with minimal moral accountability to God, much less to each other.

The absence of church discipline is no longer remarkable—it is generally not even noticed. Regulative and restorative church discipline is, to many church members, no longer a meaningful category, or even a memory. The present generation of both ministers and church members is virtually without experience of biblical church discipline.

As a matter of fact, most Christians introduced to the biblical teaching concerning church discipline—the third mark of the church—confront the issue of church discipline as an idea they have never before encountered. At first hearing, the issue seems as antiquarian and foreign as the Spanish Inquisition and the Salem witch trials. Their only acquaintance with the disciplinary ministry of the church is often a literary invention such as *The Scarlet Letter.*

And yet, without a recovery of functional church discipline—firmly established upon the principles revealed in the Bible—the church will continue its slide into moral dissolution and relativism. Evangelicals have long recognized discipline as the "third mark" of the authentic church. Authentic biblical discipline is not an elective, but a necessary and integral mark of authentic Christianity.

How did this happen? How could the church so quickly and pervasively abandon one of its most essential functions and responsibilities? The answer is found in developments both internal and external to the church.

Put simply, the abandonment of church discipline is

linked to American Christianity's creeping accommodation to American culture. As the twentieth century began, this accommodation became increasingly evident as the church acquiesced to a culture of moral individualism.

Though the nineteenth century was not a golden era for American evangelicals, the century did see the consolidation of evangelical theology and church patterns. Manuals of church discipline and congregational records indicate that discipline was regularly applied. Protestant congregations exercised discipline as a necessary and natural ministry to the members of the church, and as a means of protecting the doctrinal and moral integrity of the congregation.

As ardent congregationalists, the Baptists left a particularly instructive record of nineteenth-century discipline. Historian Gregory A. Wills aptly commented, "To an antebellum Baptist, a church without discipline would hardly have counted as a church."[1] Churches held regular "days of discipline," when the congregation would gather to heal breaches of fellowship, admonish wayward members, rebuke the obstinate, and, if necessary, excommunicate those who resisted discipline. In so doing,

---

1. Gregory A. Wills, *Democratic Religion: Freedom, Authority, and Church Discipline in the Baptist South, 1785-1900* (New York: Oxford University Press, 1997), 12.

congregations understood themselves to be following a biblical pattern laid down by Christ and the apostles for the protection and correction of disciples.

No sphere of life was considered outside the congregation's accountability. Members were to conduct their lives and witness in harmony with the Bible and with established moral principles. Depending on the denominational polity, discipline was codified in church covenants, books of discipline, congregational manuals, and confessions of faith. Discipline covered both doctrine and conduct. Members were disciplined for behavior that violated biblical principles or congregational covenants, but also for violations of doctrine and belief. Members were considered to be under the authority of the congregation and accountable to each other.

By the turn of the century, however, church discipline was already on the decline. In the wake of the Enlightenment, criticism of the Bible and the doctrines of evangelical orthodoxy was widespread. Even the most conservative denominations began to show evidence of decreased attention to theological orthodoxy. At the same time, the larger culture moved toward the adoption of autonomous moral individualism. The result of these internal and external developments was the abandonment of church discipline as ever larger portions of the church member's life were considered off-limits to the congregation.

This great shift in church life followed the tremendous cultural transformations of the early twentieth century—an era of "progressive" thought and moral liberalization. By the 1960s, only a minority of churches even pretended to practice regulative church discipline. Significantly, confessional accountability and moral discipline were generally abandoned together.

The theological category of sin has been replaced, in many circles, with the psychological concept of therapy. As Philip Rieff has argued, the "Triumph of the Therapeutic" is now a fixture of modern American culture.[2] Church members may make poor choices, fail to live up to the expectations of an oppressive culture, or be inadequately self-actualized—but they no longer sin.

Individuals now claim an enormous zone of personal privacy and moral autonomy. The congregation—redefined as a mere voluntary association—has no right to intrude into this space. Many congregations have forfeited any responsibility to confront even the most public sins of their members. Consumed with pragmatic methods of church growth and congregational engineering, most

---

2. Philip Rieff, *The Triumph of the Therapeutic: Uses of Faith after Freud* (New York: Harper and Row, 1966).

churches leave moral matters to the domain of the individual conscience.

As Thomas Oden notes, the confession of sin is now passé and hopelessly outdated to many minds:

> Naturalistic reductionism has invited us to reduce alleged individual sins to social influences for which individuals are not responsible. Narcissistic hedonism has demeaned any talk of sin or confession as ungratifying and dysfunctional. Autonomous individualism has divorced sin from a caring community. Absolute relativism has regarded moral values as so ambiguous that there is no measuring rod against which to assess anything as sin. Thus modernity, which is characterized by the confluence of these four ideological streams, has presumed to do away with confession, and has in fact made confession an embarrassment to the accommodating church of modernity.[3]

The very notion of shame has been discarded by a generation for which shame is an unnecessary and repres-

---

3. Thomas C. Oden, *Corrective Love: The Power of Communion Discipline* (St. Louis: Concordia, 1995), 56.

sive hindrance to personal fulfillment. Even secular observers have noted the shamelessness of modern culture. As James Twitchell comments:

> We have in the last generation tried to push shame aside. The human-potential and recovered-memory movements in psychology; the moral relativism of audience-driven Christianity; the penalty-free, all-ideas-are-equally-good transformation in higher education; the rise of no-fault behavior before the law; the often outrageous distortions in the telling of history so that certain groups can feel better about themselves; and the "I'm shame-free, but you should be ashamed of yourself" tone of political discourse are just some of the instances wherein this can be seen.[4]

Twitchell sees the Christian church aiding and abetting this moral transformation and abandonment of shame—which is, after all, a natural product of sinful behavior. "Looking at the Christian Church today, you can only see a dim pentimento of what was once painted in the boldest of colors.... Christianity has simply lost *it.*

---

4. James B. Twitchell, *For Shame: The Loss of Common Decency in American Culture* (New York: St. Martin's Press, 1997), 35.

It no longer articulates the ideal. Sex is on the loose. Shame days are over. The Devil has absconded with sin." As Twitchell laments, "Go and sin no more" has been replaced with "Judge not lest you be judged."[5]

Demonstration of this moral abandonment is seen in mainline Protestantism's surrender to an ethic of sexual "liberation." Liberal Protestantism has lost any moral credibility in the sexual sphere. Homosexuality is not condemned, even though it is clearly condemned in the Bible. To the contrary, homosexuals get a special caucus at the denominational assembly and their own publications and special rights.

Evangelicals, though still claiming adherence to biblical standards of morality, have overwhelmingly capitulated to the divorce culture. Where are the evangelical congregations that hold married couples accountable for maintaining their marriage vows? To a great extent, evangelicals are just slightly behind liberal Protestantism in accommodating to the divorce culture and accepting what amounts to "serial monogamy"—faithfulness to one marital partner *at a time.* This, too, has been noted by secular observers. David Blankenhorn of the Institute for American Values remarked:

---

5. Twitchell, *For Shame,* 149.

Over the past three decades, many religious leaders…have largely abandoned marriage as a vital area of religious attention, essentially handing the entire matter over to opinion leaders and divorce lawyers in the secular society. Some members of the clergy seem to have lost interest in defending and strengthening marriage. Others report that they worry about offending members of their congregations who are divorced or unmarried.[6]

Tied to this worry about offending church members is the rise of the "rights culture," which understands society only in terms of individual rights rather than moral responsibility. Mary Ann Glendon of the Harvard Law School documents the substitution of "rights talk" for moral discourse.[7] Unable or unwilling to deal with moral categories, modern men and women resort to the only moral language they know and understand—the unembarrassed claim to "rights" that society has no authority to limit or deny. This "rights talk" is not limited to secular society, however. Church members are so committed to

---

6. David Blankenhorn, *Fatherless America: Confronting Our Most Urgent Social Problem* (New York: BasicBooks, 1995), 231.

7. Mary Ann Glendon, *Rights Talk: The Impoverishment of Political Discourse* (New York: Free Press, 1991).

their own version of "rights talk" that some congregations accept almost any behavior, belief, or "lifestyle" as acceptable, or at least off-limits to congregational sanction.

The result of this is the loss of the biblical pattern for the church and the impending collapse of authentic Christianity in this generation. As Carl Laney laments:

> The church today is suffering from an infection which has been allowed to fester.... As an infection weakens the body by destroying its defense mechanisms, so the church has been weakened by this ugly sore. The church has lost its power and effectiveness in serving as a vehicle for social, moral, and spiritual change. This illness is due, at least in part, to a neglect of church discipline.[8]

The mandate of the church is to maintain true gospel doctrine and order. A church lacking these essential qualities is, biblically defined, not a true church. That is a hard word, for it clearly indicts thousands of American congregations that long ago abandoned this essential mark and have accommodated themselves to the spirit of

---

8. J. Carl Laney, *A Guide to Church Discipline: God's Loving Plan for Restoring Believers to Fellowship with Himself and with the Body of Christ* (Minneapolis: Bethany House, 1985), 12.

the age. Fearing lawsuits and lacking courage, these churches allow sin to go unconfronted and heresy to grow unchecked.

John Leadley Dagg, the author of a well-known and influential church manual of the nineteenth century, noted, "It has been remarked, that when discipline leaves a church, Christ goes with it."[9] If so, and I fear it must be so, Christ has abandoned many churches that are blissfully unaware of His departure.

---

9. J. L. Dagg, *Manual of Theology: A Treatise on Church Order* (Charleston, SC: The Southern Baptist Publication Society, 1858), 274.

16

THE DEMISE OF CHURCH DISCIPLINE, PART 2

The disappearance of church discipline has weakened the church and compromised Christian witness. The church's abdication of its moral responsibility has also led to public humiliation before the watching world. Any road to recovery will take the church through a rediscovery of the biblical and theological foundations for congregational discipline. The integrity of the people of God should always be a paramount concern. This story does not begin with the church, but with Israel.

Throughout the Bible, the people of God are characterized by a distinctive purity. This moral purity is not their own achievement, but the work of God within their midst. As the Lord spoke to the children of Israel: "For I am the LORD your God. Consecrate yourselves therefore, and be holy, for I am holy" (Leviticus 11:44). Given that they have been chosen by a holy God as a people of His own name, God's chosen people are to reflect His holiness by their way of living, worship, and beliefs.

The holiness code is central to the understanding of the Old Testament. As God's chosen nation, Israel must live by God's Word and Law, which will set the children of Israel visibly apart from their pagan neighbors. As the Lord spoke through Moses: "You should diligently keep the commandments of the LORD your God, and His testimonies and His statutes which He has commanded you. You shall do what is right and good in the sight of the LORD, that it may be well with you and that you may go in and possess the good land which the LORD swore to give your fathers" (Deuteronomy 6:17–18).

The nation is reminded that it is now known by God's name and is to reflect His holiness. "For you are a holy people to the LORD your God; the LORD your God has chosen you to be a people for His own possession out of all the peoples who are on the face of the earth" (Deuteronomy 7:6). God promised His covenant faithfulness to His people, but expected them to obey His Word and follow His Law. Israel's judicial system was largely designed to protect the purity of the nation.

In the New Testament, the church is likewise described as the people of God, who are visible to the world by their purity of life and integrity of testimony. As Peter instructed the church: "But you are a chosen race, a royal priesthood, a holy nation, a people for God's own possession, so that you may proclaim the excellencies of Him who has called you out of darkness into His marvelous light; for once you were not a people, but now you are the people of God; you had not received mercy, but now you have received mercy" (1 Peter 2:9–10).

Peter continued: "Beloved, I urge you as aliens and strangers to abstain from fleshly lusts which wage war against the soul. Keep your behavior excellent among the Gentiles, so that in the thing in which they slander you as evildoers, they may because of your good deeds, as they observe them, glorify God in the day of visitation" (1 Peter 2:11–12).

As the new people of God, the church is to see itself as an alien community in the midst of spiritual darkness—strangers to the world who must abstain from the lusts and enticements of the world. The church is to be conspicuous in its purity and holiness and steadfast in its confession of the faith once for all delivered to the saints. Rather than capitulating to the moral (or immoral) environment, Christians are to be conspicuous by their good behavior. As Peter summarized: "Like the Holy One who called you, be holy yourselves also in all your behavior" (1 Peter 1:15).

The apostle Paul clearly linked the holiness expected of believers to the completed work of Christ in redemption: "And although you were formerly alienated and hostile in mind, engaged in evil deeds, yet He has now reconciled you in His fleshly body through death, in order to present you before Him holy and blameless and beyond reproach" (Colossians 1:21–22). Clearly, this holiness made complete in the believer is the work of God, and holiness is the evidence of that redemptive work. To the Corinthian congregation, Paul urged: "Let us cleanse ourselves from all defilement of flesh and spirit, perfecting holiness in the fear of God" (2 Corinthians 7:1).

The identity of the church as the people of God is to be evident in its pure confession of Christ, its bold testimony to the gospel, and its moral holiness before the watching world. Nothing less will mark the church as the true vessel of the gospel.

The first dimension of discipline in the church is that discipline exercised directly by God as He deals with believers. As the book of Hebrews warns:

You have forgotten the exhortation which is addressed to you as sons, "My son, do not regard lightly the discipline of the Lord, nor faint when you are reproved by Him; for those whom the Lord loves He disciplines, and He scourges every son whom He receives." It is for discipline that you endure; God deals with you as with sons; for what son is there whom his father does not discipline? (Hebrews 12:5–7)

As the passage continues, the author warns that those who are without discipline "are illegitimate children and not sons" (Hebrews 12:8). The purpose of discipline, however, is righteousness: "All discipline for the moment seems not to be joyful, but sorrowful; yet to those who have been trained by it, afterwards it yields the peaceful fruit of righteousness" (Hebrews 12:11).

God's loving discipline of His people is His sovereign right and is completely in keeping with His moral character—His own holiness. His fatherly discipline also establishes the authority and pattern for discipline in the church. Correction is for the greater purpose of restoration and the even higher purpose of reflecting the holiness of God.

The second dimension of discipline in the church is that disciplinary responsibility addressed to the church itself. Like God's fatherly discipline of those He loves, the church is to exercise discipline as an integral part of its moral and theological responsibility. That the church can fall into moral disrepute is evident in the New Testament itself.

The apostle Paul confronted a case of gross moral failure in the Corinthian congregation that included "immorality of such a kind as does not exist even among the Gentiles" (1 Corinthians 5:1). In this case, apparent incest was known to the congregation, and yet it had taken no action.

"You have become arrogant and have not mourned instead, so that the one who had done this deed would be removed from your midst," Paul accused the Corinthian congregation (1 Corinthians 5:2). He instructed them to act quickly and boldly to remove this stain from their fellowship. He also warned them: "Your boasting is not good. Do you not know that a little leaven leavens the whole lump of dough? Clean out the old leaven so that you may be a new lump, just as you are in fact unleavened" (1 Corinthians 5:6–7).

Paul is outraged that the Corinthian Christians would tolerate this horrible sin. Incest, though not literally unknown in the pagan world, was universally condemned and not tolerated. In this respect, the Corinthian church had fallen beneath the moral standards of the pagan world to whom they were to witness. Paul was also exasperated with a congregation he had already warned. Mentioning an earlier letter unavailable to us, Paul scolded the Corinthians:

> I wrote you in my letter not to associate with immoral people; I did not at all mean with the immoral people of this world, or with the covetous and swindlers, or with idolaters, for then you would have to go out of the world. But actually, I wrote to you not to associate with any so-called brother if he is an immoral person, or covetous, or an idolater, or a reviler, or a drunkard, or a swindler—not even to eat with such a one. For what have I to do with judging outsiders? Do you not judge those who are within the church? But those who are outside, God judges. Remove the wicked man from among yourselves. (1 Corinthians 5:9–13)

The moral outrage of a wounded apostle is evident in these pointed verses, which called the Corinthian church to action and the exercise of discipline. They had now fallen into corporate sin by tolerating the presence of such a bold and arrogant sinner in their midst. Their moral testimony is clouded, and their fellowship is impure.

Their arrogance has blinded them to the offense they have committed before the Lord. The open sin in their midst is like a cancer that, left unchecked, will spread throughout the entire body.

The apostle's concern about the Corinthian church is a startling catalyst for concern about today's congregations, many of which are following a Corinthian pattern of moral compromise. Paul's letter is a poignant reminder of what is at stake in the recovery of biblical church discipline—nothing less than the church's witness before the world.

17

THE DEMISE OF CHURCH DISCIPLINE, PART 3

n 1 Corinthians 5, the apostle Paul confronted a case of gross moral failure in the Corinthian church. In the face of such sin, however, the church had done nothing. So how should the Corinthians have responded to this public sin? Paul wrote in this passage of delivering this sinner unto Satan and removing him from fellowship. How is this to be done? To the Galatians Paul wrote that "if anyone is caught in any trespass, you who are spiritual, restore such a one in a spirit of gentleness; each one looking to yourself, so that you too will not be tempted" (Galatians 6:1). This teaching is clear, indicating that spiritual leaders of the church are to confront a sinning member with a spirit of humility and gentleness, and with the goal of restoration. But what are the precise steps to be taken?

The Lord Himself provided these instructions as He taught His disciples:

> If your brother sins, go and show him his fault in private; if he listens to you, you have won your brother. But if he does not listen to you, take one or two more with you, so that by the mouth of two or three witnesses every fact may be confirmed. If he refuses to listen to them, tell it to the church; and if he refuses to listen even to the church, let him be to you as a Gentile and a tax collector." (Matthew 18:15–17)

The Lord instructed His disciples that they should first confront a sinning brother in private. "Show him his fault," instructed the Lord. If the brother acknowledges the sin and repents, the brother has been won. The fact that the first step is a private confrontation is very important. This limits the injury caused by the sin, and avoids a public spectacle, which would tarnish the witness of the church to the gospel.

In the event the private confrontation does not lead to repentance, restoration, and reconciliation, the next step is to take witnesses. Jesus cited the Deuteronomic Law, which required multiple witnesses of a crime for conviction. Yet His purpose seems larger than the mere establishment of the facts of the case. Jesus seems to intend for the witnesses to be an important presence in the event of the confrontation, thus adding corroborating testimony concerning the confrontation of a sinning brother. The brother cannot claim that he was not confronted with his sin in a brotherly context.

If the brother does not listen even in the presence of one or two witnesses, this becomes a matter for the congregation. "Tell it to the church," instructed Jesus, and the church is to judge the matter before the Lord, and render a judgment that is binding upon the sinner. This step is extremely serious, and the congregation now bears a corporate responsibility. The church must render its judgment based upon the principles of God's Word and the facts of the case. Again, the goal is the restoration of a sinning brother or sister—not a public spectacle.

Sadly, this congregational confrontation may not avail. If it does not, the only recourse is separation from the sinning brother. "Let him be to you as a Gentile and a tax collector," instructed the Lord, indicating that the separation is to be real and public. The congregation is not to consider the former brother as a part of the church.

This drastic and extreme act is to follow when a brother or sister will not submit to the discipline of the church. We should note that the church should still bear witness to this man, but not as a brother to a brother, until and unless repentance and restoration are evident.

What is the church's authority in church discipline? Jesus addressed this issue directly, even as He declared the establishment of the church after Peter's great confession. "I will give you the keys of the kingdom of heaven; and whatever you bind on earth shall have been bound in heaven, and whatever you loose on earth shall have been loosed in heaven" (Matthew 16:19). This "power of the keys" is one of the critical controversies between evangelicals and the Church of Rome. Roman Catholics believe that the Pope, as Peter's successor, holds these keys, and thus the power of binding and loosing. Protestants, however, believe that the Lord granted the keys to the church. This interpretation is supported by the Lord's repetition of the matter in Matthew 18:18: "Truly I say to you, whatever you bind on earth shall have been bound in heaven; and whatever you loose on earth shall have been loosed in heaven." Here, the context reveals that the power of binding and loosing is held by the church.

The terms *binding* and *loosing* were familiar terms used by rabbis in the first century to refer to the power of judging matters on the basis of the Bible. The Jewish authorities would determine how (or whether) the scriptures applied in a specific situation, and would render judgment by either "binding," which meant to restrict, or "loosing," which meant to liberate. The church still bears this responsibility and wields this power. John Calvin, the great Genevan reformer, believed that the power of "binding" should be understood as excommunication, and "loosing" as reception into membership:

> But the church binds him whom it excommunicates—not that it casts him into everlasting ruin and despair, but because it condemns his life and morals, and already warns him of his condemnation unless he should repent. It looses him whom it receives into communion, for it makes him a sharer of the unity which it has in Christ Jesus.[1]

Calvin's interpretation is fully in agreement at this point with Martin Luther, whose essay on "The Keys" (1530) is a massive refutation of papal claims and Roman Catholic tradition. Luther saw the keys as one of Christ's

---

1. John Calvin, *Institutes of the Christian Religion,* vol. 2, ed. John T. McNeill, trans. Ford Lewis Battles (Louisville, KY: Westminster John Knox Press, 1960), 1214.

great gifts to the church: "Both of these keys are extremely necessary in Christendom, so that we never can thank God enough for them." As a pastor and theologian, Luther saw the great need for the church to bear the keys, and he understood this ministry to be gracious in the recovery of sinning saints. As Luther reflected:

> For the dear Man, the faithful Bishop of our souls, Jesus Christ, is well aware that his beloved Christians are frail, that the devil, the flesh, and the world would tempt them unceasingly and in many ways, and that at times they would fall into sin. Therefore, he has given us this remedy, the key which binds, so that we might not remain too confident in our sins, arrogant, barbarous, and without God, and in the key which looses, that we should not despair in our sins.[2]

What about a church leader who sins? Paul instructed Timothy that a church leader—an elder—is "to be considered worthy of double honor" when he rules well (1 Timothy 5:17). When an elder sins, however, this is a matter of great consequence. First, no accusation is to

---

2. Martin Luther, "The Keys," in *Luther's Works*, American Edition, vol. 40, ed. Conrad Bergendoff, (Philadelphia: Fortress Press, 1958), 373.

be received on the basis of just one uncorroborated witness. If a charge is substantiated by two or three witnesses, however, the congregation is to "rebuke [him] in the presence of all, so that the rest also will be fearful of sinning" (1 Timothy 5:20). Clearly, leadership carries a higher burden, and the sins of an elder cause an even greater injury to the church. The public rebuke is necessary, for the elder sins against the entire congregation. As James warned, "Let not many of you become teachers, my brethren, knowing that as such we will incur a stricter judgment" (James 3:1).

The scandals of moral failure on the part of church leaders have caused tremendous injury to the cause of Christ. The "stricter judgment" should be a vivid warning to those who would violate the Word of God and lead others into sin by example. The failure of the contemporary church to apply consistent biblical church discipline has left most of these scandals unresolved on biblical grounds—and thus a continuing stain on the church.

18

THE DEMISE OF CHURCH DISCIPLINE, PART 4

When should the church exercise church discipline? In one sense, a form of redemptive church discipline is exercised whenever the Bible is taught and the truth of God's Word is applied to the lives of believers. The convicting power of the Word of God is the first corrective in the hearts of Christ's people. Nevertheless, a more personal and confrontational mode of discipline is required when sin threatens the faithfulness, integrity, and witness of God's people.

The Bible reveals three main areas of danger requiring discipline. These are *fidelity of doctrine, purity of life,* and *unity of fellowship.* Each is of critical and vital importance to the health and integrity of the church.

The theological confusion and compromise that mark the modern church are directly traceable to the church's failure to separate itself from doctrinal error and heretics. On this matter the Bible is clear: "Anyone who goes too far and does not abide in the teaching of Christ, does not have God; the one who abides in the teaching, he has both the Father and the Son. If anyone comes to you and does not bring this teaching, do not receive him into your house, and do not give him a greeting; for the one who gives him a greeting participates in his evil deeds" (2 John 1:9–11). The apostle Paul instructed the Galatians that "if we, or an angel from heaven, should preach to you a gospel contrary to what we have preached to you, he is to be accursed! As we have said before, so I say again now, if any man is preaching to you a gospel contrary to what you received, he is to be accursed!" (Galatians 1:8–9).

The letters of 2 Peter and Jude explicitly warn of the dangers presented to the church in the form of false prophets and heretics. Jude alerts the church that "certain persons have crept in unnoticed, those who were long beforehand marked out for this condemnation, ungodly persons who turn the grace of our God into licentiousness and deny our only Master and Lord, Jesus Christ" (Jude 1:4). Similarly, Peter warns "there will also be false teachers among you, who will secretly introduce destructive heresies, even denying the Master who bought them, bringing swift destruction upon themselves" (2 Peter 2:1).

The church must separate itself from these heresies—and from the heretics. The permissive posture of the church in this century has allowed the most heinous heresies to grow unchecked—and heretics to be celebrated. Francis Schaeffer was among the most eloquent modern prophets who decried this doctrinal cowardice. Schaeffer emphatically denied that a church could be a true Christian fellowship and allow false doctrine. As he stated:

> One cannot explain the explosive dynamite, the *dunamis,* of the early church apart from the fact that they practiced two things simultaneously: orthodoxy of doctrine and orthodoxy of community in the midst of the visible church, a community which the world could see. By the grace of God, therefore, the church must be known simultaneously for its purity of doctrine and the reality of its community.[1]

The visible community of the true church is also to be evident in its moral purity. Christians are to live in obedience to the Word of God and to be exemplary in

1. Francis A. Schaeffer, *The Church at the End of the Twentieth Century* (Wheaton, IL: Crossway, 1971), 144.

their conduct and untarnished in their testimony. A lack of attention to moral purity is a sure sign of congregational rebellion before the Lord.

Writing to the Corinthians, Paul chastised severely:

> Or do you not know that the unrighteous will not inherit the kingdom of God? Do not be deceived; neither fornicators, nor idolaters, nor adulterers, nor effeminate, nor homosexuals, nor thieves, nor the covetous, nor drunkards, nor revilers, nor swindlers, will inherit the kingdom of God. Such were some of you; but you were washed, but you were sanctified, but you were justified in the name of the Lord Jesus Christ and in the Spirit of our God. (1 Corinthians 6:9–11)

When Christians sin, their sin is to be confronted by the church in accordance with the pattern revealed in Scripture. The goal is the restoration of a sister or a brother, not the creation of a public spectacle. The greatest moral danger to the church is the toleration of sin, public and private. One of the greatest blessings to the church is the gift of biblical church discipline—the ministry of the keys.

The integrity of the church is also dependent upon

the true unity of its fellowship. Indeed, one of the most repeated warnings found in the New Testament is the admonition against toleration of schismatics. The unity of the church is one of its most visible distinctives—and its most precious gifts.

The warnings are severe: "Now I urge you, brethren, keep your eye on those who cause dissensions and hindrances contrary to the teaching which you learned, and turn away from them. For such men are slaves, not of our Lord Christ but of their own appetites; and by their smooth and flattering speech they deceive the hearts of the unsuspecting" (Romans 16:17–18). Writing to Titus, Paul instructed that the church should "reject a factious man after a first and second warning, knowing that such a man is perverted and sinning, being self-condemned" (Titus 3:10–11).

A breach in the unity of the church is a scandal in the body of Christ. The church is consistently exhorted to practice and preserve a true unity in true doctrine and biblical piety. This unity is not the false unity of a lowest-common-denominator Christianity, the "Gospel Lite" preached and taught in so many modern churches, but in the healthy and growing maturity of the congregation as it increases in grace and knowledge of the Word of God.

The ongoing function of church discipline is to be a

part of individual self-examination and congregational reflection. The importance of maintaining integrity in personal relationships was made clear by our Lord in the Sermon on the Mount, as He instructed the disciples that anger against a brother is a deadly sin. Reconciliation is a mandate—not a hypothetical goal. "Therefore if you are presenting your offering at the altar, and there remember that your brother has something against you, leave your offering there before the altar and go; first be reconciled to your brother, and then come and present your offering" (Matthew 5:23–24).

Similarly, Paul warned against participating in the Lord's Supper amidst divisions. The Supper itself is a memorial of the broken body and shed blood of the Savior, and must not be desecrated by the presence of divisions or controversies within the congregation, or by unconfessed sin on the part of individual believers.

> For as often as you eat this bread and drink the
> cup, you proclaim the Lord's death until He
> comes. Therefore whoever eats the bread or drinks
> the cup of the Lord in an unworthy manner, shall
> be guilty of the body and blood of the Lord. But
> a man must examine himself, and in so doing he
> is to eat of the bread and drink of the cup. For he

who eats and drinks, eats and drinks judgment
to himself if he does not judge the body rightly.
(1 Corinthians 11:26–29)

The "discipline of the table" is thus one of the most important disciplinary functions of the congregation. The Lord's Supper is not to be served indiscriminately, but only to those baptized believers who are under the discipline of the church and in good standing with their congregation.

In the twenty-first century, the great task of the church is to prove itself to be in continuity with the genuine church as revealed in the New Testament—proving its authenticity by a demonstration of pure faith and authentic community. We must regain the New Testament concern for fidelity of doctrine, purity of life, and unity of fellowship. We must recover the missing mark of the church.

DARKNESS AT NOON, PART 1

A Post-Christian Age

We are an affluent and comfortable people. We live in the midst of freedom as championed by those who established this nation and defined by successive generations, not only in terms of the originating vision of freedom, but now an ever-expanding understanding of liberty. We live in a time of prosperity; we live in a time of trouble. It all depends upon how you look at the world around us.

It is good for Christians to take some time to look at the trouble, for all around us are darkening skies and gathering clouds. As we engage this culture and look at it honestly, we must sense that something has happened—and is even now happening—in our culture. These major shifts will change everything we know about ministry in terms of the challenge before us and will draw out the reality of who the church is in the midst of a gathering conflict. Clouds are darkening.

We are no longer seeing the first signs of cultural trouble, but rather the indicators of advanced decay. The reality is that people now do not even know what they have lost, much less that they themselves are lost.

As a nation, we are living in the midst of an intense season of cultural, political, and moral conflict—that is no longer news. America has been through epic conflicts in the past, including a bloody civil war. Still, we must wonder if the worldview conflicts of our time may represent an even deeper conflict than those experienced in times past. We are living in a time of deep and undeniable trouble.

There is a sense, I think, in this culture that we are waiting for a signal for something to tell us which way we are going to go. Something is happening and about to happen. The landscape is changing, the skies are darkening—and this is something we know with a spiritual perception, a spiritual sense, a spiritual urgency. Something is happening that we as believers in the Lord Jesus Christ should see and understand. For we cannot say that we were not warned.

The prophet Joel declared:

I will show wonders in the heavens and on the earth, blood and fire and columns of smoke. The sun shall be turned to darkness, and the moon to blood, before the great and awesome day of the LORD comes. And it shall come to pass that everyone who calls on the name of the LORD shall be saved. For in Mount Zion and in Jerusalem there shall be those who escape, as the LORD has said, and among the survivors shall be those whom the LORD calls. (Joel 2:30–32, ESV)

And, from the book of Hebrews:

See that you do not refuse him who is speaking. For if they did not escape when they refused him who warned them on earth, much less will we escape if we reject him who warns from heaven. At that time his voice shook the earth, but now he has promised, "Yet once more I will shake not only the earth but also the heavens." This phrase, "Yet once more," indicates the removal of things that are shaken—that is, things that have been made—in order that the things that cannot be shaken may remain. Therefore let us be grateful for receiving a kingdom that cannot be shaken, and thus let us offer to God acceptable worship, with reverence and awe, for our God is a consuming fire. (Hebrews 12:25–29, ESV)

These passages describe a reality we might call "darkness at noon." In these passages we confront a prophetic vision, a prophetic warning, and a haunting reality. *Darkness at Noon*—I borrow this title from Arthur Koestler.[1] In 1941 he saw the Soviet Union in all of its horror and the Third Reich in all of its hateful fury, and he described this horrifying reality as *darkness at noon.* Our times are not the same as Koestler's, nor are the particular challenges we face. Our central concerns and fears are not represented by totalitarian governments or foreign regimes that threaten world domination, but we must see a real and present threat on our horizon. We can hear the prophet Joel—we can hear him speak of the sun turned to darkness and the moon turned to blood on the great and awful Day of the Lord. This is apocalyptic imagery—

---

1. Arthur Koestler, *Darkness at Noon,* trans. Daphne Hardy (New York: Modern Library, 1941).

we know that. It is speaking of a judgment, of a Day of the Lord that was near on Joel's horizon, and yet distant on the horizon of the eschaton, when the Lord Himself shall come to judge the living and the dead.

The imagery of judgment in this passage—of the sun turned to darkness and the moon to blood—is a foreboding image that gives us in a graphic picture a sign of the times, and around us we can see a darkening sky that threatens a darkening sun. We can see darkness at noon on the dawn.

A central dimension of this reality is the dawning of a post-Christian age. History has been altered in so many ways in the twists and turns of human experience. But who could have expected that in our times we would see those nations that once were the cradle of Christianity become so secularized that they can only be described as post-Christian in composition, in culture, in theme, and in worldview and understanding? The post-Christian sense, the post-Christian theme, the post-Christian mentality of these cultures is such that we can look to the nations of Western Europe and see what a post-Christian culture begins to look like. We hear the language, we listen to the discourse, we see the laws, we hear the judgments, we watch the culture at work, and we realize that this is what a nation, a people, an ethnos, a generation that once knew Christianity but knows it no more, looks like and sounds like. This is how they live. And it is not just Europe.

Even as demographers, pollsters, and statisticians tell us how many Americans believe in God and how many claim belief in the Lord Jesus Christ, still we can see the beginnings of a post-Christian mentality here in America. Look at the cultural elites—the political elites; the legal elites; the judicial, academic, and entertainment elites— look at them, and you will realize that they are largely post-Christian in their mentality.

The prophet Joel speaks of the "day of the Lord," when the divine judgment would fall like a terrible and swift sword. In Joel 1, the prophet wrote:

> The word of the LORD that came to Joel, the son of Pethuel: Hear this, you elders; give ear, all inhabitants of the land! Has such a thing happened in your days, or in the days of your fathers? Tell your children of it, and let your children tell their children, and their children to another generation. What the cutting locust left, the swarming locust has eaten. What the swarming locust left, the hopping locust has eaten, and what the hopping locust left, the destroying locust has eaten. (Joel 1:1–4, ESV)

This text speaks most directly of a crop, but it also points to a culture. Our culture has been savaged by locusts. What the cutting locusts leave, the swarming locusts eat. What the swarming locusts leave, the hopping locusts take. What the hopping locusts leave, the destroying locusts destroy.

We can give evidence of this in individual words, each representing an individual loss. Consider what has happened to truth, to beauty, to dignity, love, and marriage. Consider what is even now happening in our midst. We are witnessing the dawn of a post-Christian age in our own times, in our own nation, in our own world, and among our own people. We can see the ravages that will come as the sacred things are profaned and trampled underfoot. We see the evidence of this decadence and downfall in the culture—in art and music and literature. We are a people whose cultural and moral aspirations are indicated by the Neilson ratings and by the lowest common denominator of the entertainment industry. We are a nation, a people, entertained by a show called *Desperate Housewives,* by reality TV that celebrates the lowest and most base human instincts, and by entertainment that panders and is profane.

Look at what has happened to marriage and the family. The idea of romantic love is now commonly reduced to lust. We have largely destroyed the purity of marriage.

This central institution of civilization has been decried, denigrated, and even discarded. Marriage is under attack by those who would transform it into something it cannot be and never was, and truthfully never will be.

We see all of this and we wonder how it could have happened. And yet Scripture has told us that sinners love darkness rather than the light. Let me put it this way—in a truly post-Christian age, the saddest loss of all is a loss of the memory of what was lost. The saddest aspect of our dawning post-Christian age is that there is no longer even a memory of what was discarded and what was denied and rejected. Having lived for so long on the memory of Christian truth, without the substance of Christian truth, the culture now grows hostile to that truth.

Even the memory of what once was is now being lost in our generation. We are living in an age in which all constraints and restraints are to be thrown off—all in the name of the liberation that does not liberate but enslaves. We are seeing the coming of a repressive post-Christian age that is packaged as an age of unprecedented liberty. We must name it for what it is—and be aware of what a challenge this represents for the believing church.

20

DARKNESS AT NOON, PART 2

The Closing of the Postmodern Mind

The prophet Joel spoke of a day when the sun would be turned to darkness and the moon to blood. This picture—besides giving us a glimpse of that terrible, coming Day of the Lord in judgment—is also a graphic picture of our own times. Even today, in the gathering clouds of our culture, we see darkness at noon.

One of the central realities of this darkness is the dawning of a post-Christian culture—and a central reality of our emerging culture is the closing of the postmodern mind. Something is happening to the worldview, the mentality, and the consciousness of this age. If we listen closely, we can hear something like the closing of a steel door—a solemn, cataclysmic slamming of a door. We have been watching the postmodern mind in its development, and it is now well developed. Not only do we see the themes of postmodernity taking hold of the larger culture, but we understand the challenge this pattern of thinking poses to Christian truth and Christian truth-telling. Tolerance is perverted into a radical secularism that is anything but tolerant. There is little openness to truth, and growing hostility to truth claims. Indeed, the postmodern mind has a fanatical, if selective, dedication to moral relativism, and an understanding that truth has no objective or absolute basis whatsoever.

The late French philosopher Jacques Derrida shaped the postmodern mind by arguing that the author of a text is effectively dead in terms of establishing the text's meaning. One of the fathers of literary deconstructionism, his concept of "the death of the author" exerts a powerful influence on the culture at large. Derrida's basically nihilistic philosophy suggested that texts mean nothing in themselves. In other words, it is the reader who comes to the text with meaning and determines what will be found within the text. The author is dead, Derrida proclaimed, and can no longer dictate by his totalitarian authority what the text means.

Even before Derrida's death, new debates about deconstructionism arose in the academy. More significantly, these nihilistic philosophies have already filtered down into popular culture. Even now, for example, many of our judges are practicing deconstructionists, seeing the law not as what it was or what it was intended to be, but rather as a tool they can use for their own agenda of social engineering. In the elite institutions of American academia, deconstructionism is the order of the day. The text means what the professor says it means, and it eventually means whatever each student would have it to mean. The reader reigns supreme.

Unfortunately, deconstructionism has also found its way into many pulpits, sometimes in a hard, ideological form, but more often in a soft and seductive form. In the hard form of undiluted liberalism, it is simply the idea that this text, the Bible, may be a privileged text, but the authors are dead. Thus, it is now up to us to decide what it should mean, so we can turn the text on its head. And we can do so in the name of liberation and freedom from oppression. We are no longer bound to the oppressive truth of the text because we can now twist the text to mean something it has never been understood to mean in the past—even the opposite of what the words and grammatical structure would seem to mean. In so doing, postmoderns seek to liberate themselves by deconstructing the text. After all, all the authors are dead.

Of course, it is worth keeping in mind that such a hermeneutic must also assume that the divine Author is dead. In its softer, subtler form, we find deconstructionism among some who would never consider themselves liberals, and who would even claim to have what they would characterize as a high view of Scripture. Yet when they encounter the text, they also deconstruct it. The biblical text, they argue, has to be understood in terms of our modern understanding. Modern psychology, anthropology, philosophy, and cultural studies have something to bring to the interpretation of the text, they argue, something to tell us that the human authors of Scripture missed. In other words, one may start with what it said, but now we ourselves can decide what it means.

In both its hard and soft forms, deconstructionism has filtered down to the popular culture, even to those who never heard of Jacques Derrida but have been nonetheless infected with this postmodern mentality and this subtle form of subversive relativism and subjectivism. You can hear Derrida in the discourse of adolescents in the mall. You can hear it in the conversation on the nightly news.

The closing of the postmodern mind is the opposite

of what postmodernism claimed to be its aspiration. Post-modernism claimed that this new postmodern age—with the end of modernity, the demise of scientific objectivity, and the openness to new forms and understandings of truth—would lead to an opening of the mind. But as is always the case, the totalitarian opening of the mind always ends with the radical closing of the mind. There is nothing less tolerant than the modern ethos of tolerance. There is nothing less open than the modern idea of open-mindedness. In the darkening sky and the gathering clouds, we see the haunting closure of this supposedly open mind.

Sociologist Peter Berger reminds us that every single individual operates on the basis of plausibility struc-tures—certain frameworks of thought that are necessary for our understanding of the world.[1] For years, Berger and others have been telling us that the plausibility struc-tures of most Americans have little, if anything, to do with biblical Christianity. The way most persons think about the world, the way they envision beauty, the way they conceive love, the way they understand authority and marriage and structure and principle and truth, all of these things are now basically secular in form. Not only

---

1. Peter L. Berger, *The Sacred Canopy* (Garden City, NY: Doubleday, 1967).

so, but in recent years we have witnessed the acceleration of this secularism into something that is deeply dark and increasingly nihilistic. What Karl Marx once promised would happen seems to be coming to fulfillment—all that is solid melts into air. In the world of postmodernism, all institutions are plastic and all principles are liquid. We can reshape anything. Nothing is given. Nothing is objective.

We can take the family, for example, and we can melt it down and make it something else. In fact, we can turn it into an infinite number of liquid arrangements. We can take any institution, be it government or church, or marriage, or family, and we can make of it what we will. All principles are liquid, too. We can simply pour them out in a different way. Since there is nothing really there anyway, we can reconfigure any principle according to our desires. So we will reshape our entire worldview. We will shape our new philosophy. We will be humanity come of age, and we will do this in the name of liberation and tolerance and diversity—and open-mindedness. George Orwell never saw it so clearly, yet this is where we live. Openness becomes closedness. Freedom becomes bondage, and tolerance becomes intolerance.

The closing of the postmodern mind is not a pretty sight, nor is it friendly to human rights and human dignity. We can look to Europe, where the post-Christian age is already coalescing into a system of laws and a pattern of culture. Sweden, for example, already has imprisoned a Pentecostal pastor, Ake Green, for preaching a sermon in which he spoke of the sinfulness of homosexuality. He was recently acquitted of that "crime" by Sweden's highest court, but the fact remains that he was arrested and convicted by a lower court—and the law remains in effect. Across much of Western Europe there is legislation in which it is can be considered a crime to speak of the sinfulness of any sexual lifestyle, and of homosexuality in particular.

In Belgium and the Netherlands, there are now official protocols for killing children and infants in hospitals. Euthanasia has advanced to the point that, in the Netherlands, the largest medical school in the country just reported that 31 percent of pediatricians have admitted to killing babies, and 45 percent of neonatologists have admitted to euthanizing infants—even without informing the parents that that is what happened to their child.[2] And all this is done, of course, in the name of health, even in the name of compassion. Then along comes the Christian to say, "We have a message about the dignity and

2. Wesley J. Smith, "Continent Death," National Review Online, Dec. 23, 2003.

sanctity of life," and he is told to be quiet. We can say, "Well, that is Europe. That is a post-Christian future that is an ocean away."

But even in the United States, we see all this coming together, and the clenched fist of a closed postmodern mind is increasingly evident. In 1995, for instance, a U.S. District Court judge in the state of Texas ruled against school prayer, afraid that some teenagers might in the course of their graduation ceremony actually mention the name of Jesus or mention the name of God. When he handed down the ruling, the judge warned teenagers in the state of Texas, saying, "If any of you shall mention the name of Jesus or God, or any other deity, you will rue the day that you were born and will spend up to half a year in the Galveston jail." That is not Arthur Koestler warning in *Darkness at Noon* of the Soviet Union in 1941. It was the United States of America in 1995. Legal observers may argue that this judge's comments were not indicative of a universal trend, but is this truly reassuring?

In the state of California, those who would be foster parents are now required to pledge that they will say nothing that is in any way opposed to homosexuality or to any chosen sexual lifestyle. Effectively, that means that Christians can no longer be foster parents in the state of California. What a switch in ten years! Ten years ago, homosexual couples could not be foster parents in the state of California. Now it is the Christians—who would raise their children as Christians—who cannot be foster parents in that state.

A recently published book by Sam Harris titled *The End of Faith* even claimed that faith itself is a form of terrorism, and that the United States can no longer afford its long cherished ideal of religious toleration and religious liberty. According to Harris, religious liberty is simply too dangerous in a world like this.

We need to take notice of these developments in order that we might understand the challenge we are about to face, because I fear that as evangelical Christians, we tend to swing like a pendulum between a naive optimism and a wrongful pessimism. In reality, we have no right to be either optimistic or pessimistic. To be either optimistic or pessimistic is to be deluded, and in some sense to deny the sovereignty of God. We cannot be pessimistic because Scripture tells us we are to be a people of hope. Of course, that does not mean that we are a naive and ignorant people of hope who close our eyes to the reality around us. No, we find a hope in something that is far more secure than anything this culture can secure.

But, on the other hand, we cannot be optimistic either. Optimism is the message sent down from public relations. Optimism is the happy face that tells us with a chipper voice that everything is all right. Well, it is not all right, and everything will not be well, not in this age or in this life. We have no right to be optimistic, but we have no right not to be hopeful.

Evangelicals, sometimes demonstrating a nearly breathtaking naiveté, swing between these pendulum extremes of pessimism and optimism, when Scripture calls us to reality. Be sober-minded, we are told. Gird up the loins of your thinking. Be ready, be alert, be watchful. Be a watchman on the wall. Have your eyes open. Be ready for action. This is our calling as Christians, even as the darkness gathers. We are to be the community of the open-eyed, the intellectually alert, the brokenhearted, and the resolutely hopeful. Pulling that off will take more than wishful thinking.

21

DARKNESS AT NOON, PART 3

The Commission of a Post-Compliant Church

As the late Allan Bloom noted, a mind resolutely determined to be absolutely open is often, in actuality, quite closed.[1] The closing of the postmodern mind will present a challenge for the church in this post-Christian age. Swirling worldviews and a reflexive relativism come together to form a mentality often closed to all substantive truth-claims. Gathering clouds of darkness and the eclipse of truth present the believing church with a great

---

1. Alan Bloom, *The Closing of the American Mind* (New York: Touchstone, 1987).

challenge—will we surrender in a spirit of cultural compliance?

We must recognize that the church has been compliant for far too long, and if we are effectively to challenge the prevailing worldview of postmodern culture, the church must become a *post*-compliant people. What will it take for Christians in this generation to be awakened out of complacency and compliance? If we are complacent in this culture, if we are compliant in the face of its demands and expectations, then there will be no preaching of the gospel. There will be no authentic church. There will be no authentic Christian witness. We will withdraw into our Christian cave, and we will cower there. We will not witness, we will not work—we will simply retreat.

A recent debate between Robert Audi and Nicholas Wolterstorff is very revealing. In a book entitled *Religion in the Public Square,* Robert Audi takes the secular argument—which is the prevalent position in the academy—and argues that Christians have no right to make Christian arguments in the public square. It is fine for Christians to make *arguments,* he says; they just cannot show up *as Christians.* Following in the work of the philosopher John Rawls, Audi goes so far as to say that when we enter the public square, we must bring with us a purely *secular rationale.* In other words, any argument we make must be essentially and purely secular, and such arguments are to be motivated by secular concerns *alone*. They cannot even be spiritually *motivated*.[2]

Think about what this means on the issue of homosexuality and homosexual marriage, to take just one example. I believe historians will one day point to this issue as the catalyst for a great and lamentable cultural revolution in America. The world will be categorically different the moment homosexual marriage is normalized in this country. Then we will find out how many Christians there are. We will find out how many churches there are. Who is going to recognize these same-sex unions? Who is going to solemnize these same-sex unions? Not the faithful church of the Lord Jesus Christ! Any church that would normalize and celebrate what Scripture condemns has set itself in direct opposition to revelation, reason, and the witness of the martyrs. Those who gave their lives for the sake of the gospel did not do so in a spirit of cultural compliance.

Think for a moment about this issue of same-sex marriage in the context of Audi's *secular rationale*. I was in Washington recently and heard a presentation in which a

2. Robert Audi and Nicholas Wolterstorff, *Religion in the Public Square: The Place of Religious Convictions in Public Debate* (New York: Rowman and Littlefield, 1997).

very well-informed person—one of the nation's leading researchers on the issues of the day—said, "Look, we have to understand that we are not going to be able to bring God into the same-sex marriage debate. We are not going to be able to use spiritual and biblical arguments, so you Christian people are just going to have to understand that." I was up next to speak, so I said in response, "Here is everything I know about marriage apart from God— nothing of binding significance. Now that that is out of the way, I can tell you that everything I know about marriage, everything I know about sex, everything I know about gender, everything I know about homosexuality, I know from the Word of God. That is all I know. That is all I *can* know, and I am not going to *not* talk about it. And if we lose this battle while preaching the Scriptures, then brothers and sisters, we lose gloriously!"

There are many who will say that what must be pressed in this debate over same-sex marriage are the deleterious social effects of undermining marriage—and leave all theologically based arguments out of the picture. That argument, however, is not only wrong in principle, but it is a pragmatic failure. We will never get anywhere with that, because the people driving the movement for normalizing homosexuality really aren't primarily concerned about those issues. A culture that will compromise itself into accepting homosexual marriage will never really be convinced by such arguments. In the final analysis, all we have is the authority of the Word of God. We Christians are the world's most eccentric people in a postmodern age. We are committed to a faith that is structured by a book that is two thousand years old. Beyond eccentric, we are increasingly seen as *dangerous.* A people who live by the light of an ancient book—and who dare to call it the very Word of God—will look exceedingly dangerous to the prevailing worldviews of this age.

The entire biblical truth-claim is under assault in today's culture. We see the tightening grip in the tenacity of all this onslaught. We see a culture that increasingly loves darkness rather than the light. We can see the logic of the culture, and we can see that the church has been compliant too long. Thus, when we turn to Hebrews 12, we are confronted with an exhortation that instructs us that the reality must be different for us. The prophet Joel warned of that apocalyptic day of judgment that is coming—a day when the sun will turn to darkness and the moon will be turned to blood. In Hebrews 12, we are confronted with another warning of judgment—this time addressed to the church of the Lord Jesus Christ. The writer of Hebrews writes of two mountains, Mount Sinai and Mount Zion. One represents the covenant of old, and the other represents the New Covenant in Christ. Sinai represents thunder and shaking and fear; Zion represents the festive joy of the people of God in the work of Christ, in the kingdom of the Redeemer.

In this passage, we are also told of a shaking that is about to come. In Hebrews 12:26, the author quoted from the prophet Haggai in chapter 2, verses 6–7: "For thus says the LORD of hosts, 'Once more in a little while, I am going to shake the heavens and the earth, the sea also and the dry land. I will shake all the nations; and they will come with the wealth of all nations, and I will fill this house with glory,' says the LORD of hosts." Then the writer of Hebrews picked up by saying, "This expression, 'Yet once more,' denotes the removing of those things which can be shaken, as of created things, so that those things which cannot be shaken may remain" (Hebrews 12:27).

We are now in a time of shaking, and there is more shaking yet to come. As we read the book of Hebrews, this too is pointing toward an eschatological shaking and sifting. But just as in Joel, there is both an eschatological and a present application. There is a shaking now happening in this generation, and this shaking will be followed by more and more violent shaking yet. We are about to see what remains and what falls. In this time of shifting and sifting and shaking, we are going to be tested, and we are going to find out what we are made of.

Look at Hebrews 12:28–29: "Therefore, since we receive a kingdom which cannot be shaken, let us show gratitude, by which we may offer to God an acceptable service with reverence and awe; for our God is a consuming fire." Let us be grateful for receiving a kingdom that cannot be shaken. Yes, there is a whole lot of shaking going on! But there is one kingdom that cannot be shaken, and that is the kingdom of our Lord Jesus Christ.

What does that kingdom look like? It is certainly a kingdom of victory, but it is sometimes a victory that doesn't look to observers like victory. Look at Hebrews 11:32–38:

> And what more shall I say? For time will fail me
> if I tell of Gideon, Barak, Samson, Jephthah, of
> David and Samuel and the prophets, who by faith
> conquered kingdoms, performed acts of righteous-
> ness, obtained promises, shut the mouths of lions,
> quenched the power of fire, escaped the edge of
> the sword, from weakness were made strong,
> became mighty in war, put foreign armies to flight.
> Women received back their dead by resurrection;
> and others were tortured, not accepting their

release, so that they might obtain a better resurrection; and others experienced mockings and scourgings, yes, also chains and imprisonment. They were stoned, they were sawn in two, they were tempted, they were put to death with the sword; they went about in sheepskins, in goatskins, being destitute, afflicted, ill-treated (men of whom the world was not worthy), wandering in deserts and mountains and caves and holes in the ground.

I think it is fair to say that to the casual, outside observer, this picture does not look much like victory. But in the eyes of faith, it doesn't get any more victorious than what this passage declares. We don't get to choose our times. We don't get to choose our challenges. We didn't choose to live in a post-Christian age. We didn't choose to confront the postmodern mind, but this is where we are, and it is time that we become a post-compliant church. While all is shaking and shaken around us, the one thing that cannot be shaken is the kingdom of our Lord Jesus Christ, and this kingdom is visible in His church.

In a post-Christian age, confronted with the challenge of the postmodern mind, the church of the Lord Jesus Christ is called to be a post-compliant people. Anything less is just another form of spiritual surrender.

22

MISSIONS AT RISK

A Failure of Nerve

America's evangelical Christians are facing a critical testing-time in the twenty-first century. Among the most important of the tests we now face is the future of missions and our faithfulness to the Great Commission. At a time of unprecedented opportunity, will our zeal for world missions slacken?

Just as doors of opportunity are opening around the world, the church seems to be losing its voice. A virtual repaganization of Western culture is occurring, indicating that the failure of the American church is evident at home as well as abroad. What is the root issue?

At base, the issue is a failure of theological nerve—a devastating loss of biblical and doctrinal conviction. The result is retreat on the mission fields of the world and regression on the home front. Since the middle of the last century, the mainline Protestant denominations have been withdrawing from the missionary enterprise, some even declaring a "moratorium" on the sending of missionaries charged to preach the gospel. Among these denominations, the total missionary force is now a fraction of that during the 1950s, and many of those who remain on the fields have been assigned duties far removed from conversionist witness.

This loss of theological nerve is a fundamental failure of conviction. Put bluntly, many who claim to be Christians simply do not believe that anyone is actually lost.

The essence of this belief is universalism, the belief that all persons will be saved, whether or not they have a saving relationship with Jesus Christ. Universalism presents itself in many forms, including modern inclusivism, pluralism, and relativism. In its boldest and most honest form, it is the absolute declaration that all persons will be saved (if indeed there is anything from which to be saved). By this account, all religions have an equal claim to truth that underlies the "religious" character of humanity.

In its more romanticized forms, universalism is the belief that God would not actually sentence rebellious human beings to eternal punishment, in spite of what He reveals in Holy Scripture. These persons believe in a God of their own devising, and not the God of the Bible.

Universalism also presents itself in a naive form, in which Christians refuse to deal with the issue and simply declare no position or conviction on the issue. Their stance betrays their lack of conviction and even compassion. Their conscience is uncluttered by concern for the lost.

The believing church down through the ages has steadfastly resisted the universalist temptation, because universalism is so directly opposed to the clear teaching of Scripture. The Bible presents Jesus Christ and His atoning work as the only means of salvation, His gospel as the only "good news" for a lost world, and the gospel as the global mandate of the church.

There is no room for universalism—whatever its form—in evangelical churches. By rejecting the finality of Jesus Christ and the integrity of His gospel, those who promote universalism are witnesses to another gospel—demonstrating a perversion of the gospel just as the apostle Paul warned.

Given their commitment to the gospel, could evangelical Christians allow universalism to make inroads into their ranks? There are signs that this is now well under way. In the evangelical academy, some are advocating views well in line with the liberal Protestant arguments of the midcentury. The challenge of pluralism has found many evangelicals with weak knees. The pattern of evangelical compromise is also evident in those who seek to reduce the unique claim Christianity makes to truth, and also among those who promote the idea of a second opportunity for saving faith after death.

The pattern is not restricted to the academics, however. The most dangerous trend may be found in the pews of evangelical churches, where more and more Christians are willing to reject or compromise the uniqueness of Christ and His atonement, citing the apparent "sincerity" of those who worship other gods, or no god at all. Many American Christians seem increasingly reluctant to believe that their unsaved neighbors will go to hell. The urgency of world missions is a strange concept to a generation seemingly preoccupied with feel-good religion and self-help courses.

Where will the church stand? A report released just a few years ago indicated that only a third of the participants at an Urbana missions conference (bringing together thousands of college-aged evangelicals) indicated a belief that "a person who does not hear the gospel is eternally lost." As one missionary veteran responded: "If two-thirds of the most missions-minded young people in

America do not affirm the lostness of mankind, the Great Commission is in serious trouble!" Should these trends remain unchecked and uncorrected, the missions cause—and the church itself—will be in serious trouble indeed.

This is, as the late Carl F. H. Henry advised, a time for evangelical demonstration.[1] Our words of support for the missionary cause are meaningless if we do not produce a new generation of bold, courageous, and committed Christian missionaries. Let us make our convictions clear. Evangelical Christians must take our stand for the gospel of the Lord Jesus Christ, who alone has made atonement for our sins. In a day of pluralism, we must point to the only gospel that offers salvation. We must learn again to define the true gospel in terms of justification by grace alone, through faith alone, in Christ alone. This is the sum and substance of the genuine gospel—and the true gospel is always a missionary gospel.

---

1. Carl F. H. Henry, *A Plea for Evangelical Demonstration* (Grand Rapids, MI: Baker Books, 1971).

23

THE URGENCY
OF PREACHING

Has preaching fallen on hard times? An open debate is now being waged over the character and centrality of preaching in the church. At stake is nothing less than the integrity of Christian worship and proclamation.

How did this happen? Given the central place of preaching in the New Testament church, it would seem that the priority of biblical preaching should be uncontested. After all, as John A. Broadus—one of the great preachers of Christian history—famously remarked, "Preaching is characteristic of Christianity. No false religion has ever provided for the regular and frequent assembling of the masses of men, to hear religious instruction and exhortation."[1]

---

1. John Broadus, *A Treatise on the Preparation and Delivery of Sermons* (1870; repr., New York: Harper and Brothers Publishers, 1926), 1.

Yet numerous influential voices within evangelicalism suggest that the age of the expository sermon is now past. In its place, some contemporary preachers now substitute messages intentionally designed to reach secular or superficial congregations—messages that avoid preaching a biblical text, and thus avoid a potentially embarrassing confrontation with biblical truth.

A subtle shift visible at the onset of the twentieth century became a great divide as the century ended. The shift from expository preaching to more topical and human-centered approaches has grown into a debate over the place of Scripture in preaching, and the nature of preaching itself.

Two famous statements about preaching illustrate this growing divide. Reflecting poetically on the urgency and centrality of preaching, the Puritan pastor Richard Baxter once remarked, "I Preach'd, as never sure to Preach again, and as a dying man to dying men."[2] With vivid expression and a sense of gospel gravity, Baxter understood that preaching is literally a life-or-death affair. Eternity hangs in the balance as the preacher proclaims the Word.

Contrast that statement to the words of Harry Emerson Fosdick, perhaps the most famous (or infamous)

---

2. Richard Baxter, *Poetical Fragments* (J. Dunton, 1689), 30.

preacher of the twentieth century's early decades. Fosdick, pastor of the Riverside Church in New York City, provided an instructive contrast to the venerable Baxter. "Preaching," he explained, "should be personal counseling on a group scale."[3]

These two statements about preaching reveal the contours of the contemporary debate. For Baxter, the promise of heaven and the horrors of hell frame the preacher's consuming burden. For Fosdick, the preacher is a kindly counselor offering helpful advice and encouragement.

The current debate over preaching is most commonly explained as an argument about the focus and shape of the sermon. Should the preacher seek to preach a biblical text through an expository sermon? Or, should the preacher direct the sermon to the "felt needs" and perceived concerns of the hearers?

Clearly, many evangelicals now favor the second approach. Urged on by devotees of "needs-based preaching," many evangelicals have abandoned the text without recognizing that they have done so. These preachers may eventually get to the text in the course of the sermon, but the text does not set the agenda or establish the shape of the message.

---

3. Harry Emerson Fosdick, *The Living of These Days* (New York: Harper and Brothers, 1956), 94.

Focusing on so-called perceived needs and allowing these needs to set the preaching agenda inevitably leads to a loss of biblical authority and biblical content in the sermon. Yet, this pattern is increasingly the norm in many evangelical pulpits. Fosdick must be smiling from the grave.

Earlier evangelicals recognized Fosdick's approach as a rejection of biblical preaching. An out-of-the-closet theological liberal, Fosdick paraded his rejection of biblical inspiration, inerrancy, and infallibility—and rejected other doctrines central to the Christian faith. Enamored with trends in psychological theory, Fosdick became liberal Protestantism's happy pulpit therapist. The goal of his preaching was well captured by the title of one of his many books, *On Being a Real Person.*

Shockingly, this is now the approach evident in many evangelical pulpits. The sacred desk has become an advice center and the pew has become the therapist's couch. Psychological and practical concerns have displaced theological exegesis and the preacher directs his sermon to the congregation's perceived needs.

The problem is, of course, that the sinner does not know what his most urgent need is. She is blind to her need for redemption and reconciliation with God and focuses on potentially real but temporal needs such as personal fulfillment, financial security, family peace, and career advancement. Too many sermons settle for answering these expressed needs and concerns, and fail to proclaim the Word of Truth.

Without doubt, few preachers following this popular trend intend to depart from the Bible. But under the guise of an intention to reach modern secular men and women "where they are," the sermon has been transformed into a success seminar. Some verses of Scripture may be added to the mix, but for a sermon to be genuinely biblical, the text must set the agenda as the foundation of the message—not as an authority cited for spiritual footnoting.

Charles Spurgeon confronted the very same pattern of wavering pulpits in his own day. Some of the most fashionable and well-attended London churches featured pulpiteers who were the precursors to modern needs-based preachers. Spurgeon—who managed to draw a few thousand hearers each service despite his insistence on biblical preaching—confessed, "The true ambassador for Christ feels that he himself stands before God, and has to deal with souls in God's stead as God's servant, and... stands in a solemn place—a place in which unfaithfulness is inhumanity to man as well as treason to God."[4]

---

4. C. H. Spurgeon, "Negotiations for Peace: A Sermon Delivered on the Lord's-Day Evening, September 18, 1870," in *The Metropolitan Tabernacle Pulpit,* vol. 16 (Pasadena, TX: Pilgrim Publications, 1983).

Spurgeon and Baxter understood the dangerous mandate of the preacher, and were therefore driven to the Bible as their only authority and message. They left their pulpits trembling with urgent concern for the souls of their hearers and fully aware of their accountability to God for preaching His Word, and His Word alone. Their sermons were measured by power; Fosdick's by popularity.

Authentic expository preaching takes the presentation of the Word of God as its central aim. The purpose of the preacher is to read the text, interpret the text, explain the text, and apply the text. Thus, the text drives the sermon from beginning to end. In fact, in too many of today's sermons, the text plays a subordinate role to other concerns.

Real exposition takes time, preparation, dedication, and discipline. The foundation of expository preaching is the confidence that the Holy Spirit will apply the Word to the hearts of the hearers—explained by the Reformers as the ministry of Word and Spirit. That ministry—so vital to the people of God—is missing or minimized in many evangelical congregations.

The current debate over preaching may well shake congregations, denominations, and the evangelical movement. But know this: the recovery and renewal of the church in this generation will come only when from pulpit to pulpit the herald preaches as never sure to preach again, and as a dying man to dying men.